Bomber Bases of
World War 2
3rd Air Division
8th Air Force USAAF
1942–45

1

GW00537877

Bomber Bases of World War 2 3rd Air Division 8th Air Force USAAF 1942–45

Flying Fortress and Liberator Squadrons in Norfolk and Suffolk

Martin W. Bowman

Pen & Sword
AVIATION

First published in Great Britain in 2009 by
Pen & Sword Aviation
an imprint of
Pen & Sword Books Ltd

ISBN 978-1-84415-828-7

A CIP catalogue record for this book is
available from the British Library

Typeset in 10/12 Palatino by
Concept, Huddersfield, West Yorkshire

Printed and bound in England
by CPI UK

Pen & Sword Books Ltd incorporates the Imprints of Pen & Sword Aviation,
Pen & Sword Maritime, Pen & Sword Military, Wharncliffe Local History,
Pen & Sword Select, Pen & Sword Military Classics, Leo Cooper,
Remember When, Seaforth Publishing and Frontline Publishing.

For a complete list of Pen & Sword titles please contact
PEN & SWORD BOOKS LIMITED
47 Church Street, Barnsley, South Yorkshire, S70 2AS, England
E-mail: enquiries@pen-and-sword.co.uk
Website: www.pen-and-sword.co.uk

Contents

Acknowledgements

My grateful thanks are extended to: David Calcutt; Bill Carleton; Bob Collis; Clarence F. Cherry; Roy G. Davidson; Hayward F. Deese Jnr., Abe Dolim; Michael R. Downes; Michael P. Faley, 100th Bomb Group Historian; Mike Fuenfer; Joe Gualano; Larry Goldstein; Steve Gotts; the late Carlyle J. Hanson; Harry Holmes; Zdenek Hurt; Fred Huston; Wallace Johnson; Philip Kaplan; John Lindquist; Irving Lifson; Ian McLachlan; John A. Miller; Francis S. Milligan; Joseph Minton; Bryce S. Moore; Ralph J. Munn; William Nicholls; Connie and Gordon Richards; Robert J. Shoens; Griswold Smith; Richard A. Spencer; Henry Tarcza; The 95th Bomb Group Heritage Association; Thorpe Abbotts 100th Bomb Group Memorial Museum; Louis J. Torretta; Geoff Ward; Roy West.

Prologue

A bomber base is something like a little mining town back home. Each day a large part of its population sets out on the one big and dangerous job for which it exists. The rhythm of its life, like that of the mining town, follows the pace of the one industry. But there are many on the base who don't set off each day into the air, just as there are many in the town who don't go down into the earth. They are an unseen army at work on a hundred different jobs. For every bomber there are thirty or so men on the base who never fly. Some of them handle the planes on the ground, some handle the bombs, bombsights, guns, or the ever-growing battery of flying equipment. Some clothe or drive or feed the combat crews. There are many again who have less direct contact with planes or flying, but who are essential to the success of a mission.

The difference between a Group with an outstanding operational record and a run-of-the-mill outfit is as often as not the work of the unseen army and the smoothness of their teamwork with the fliers.

As a Fort or a Lib thunders down the runway in the early morning and heaves its thirty tons into the air, it carries with it the hopes and anxieties, the sweat and cursing, the patience and ingenuity of hundreds of men. It is the streamlined spearhead of months of training and experience, weeks of preparation, hours of planning. Every mission is a campaign, worked out to the last second, to the last man and to the last pound. Every mission is different, with its own problems of weather and target, route and procedure. And yet every mission follows a general pattern from the first stand-by warning to the repair of battle damage.

"Stick your nose out the door, Mac, and see if the flag's changed". Before Mac summons up the energy to roll off his bunk, Tex comes in. Yes, the blue flag is now flying, the stand-by has become an alert. "What's the time, Joe?" Joe grunts what sounds like ten-thirty. "They'll probably scrub it as soon as we get through", says Tex, "looks like rain". Tex is an armourer and a pessimist. Its nothing new to him to bomb up and unload three times in one night. Mac says nothing. He's asleep again. Why worry? They'll be routed out when they're needed. Sleep while you can, is his motto. Two weeks ago they ran eight missions in eight days and Mac, an air mechanic, averaged four-and-a-half hours sleep a night, keeping two planes flying.

While Mac and plenty of others are hitting the sack, the Operations men are just settling into their stride. Operations at headquarters gradually works up steam, until, about 4.15 in the morning, it will rival Grand Central. Right now everyone is waiting for the orders to come through from Division. As soon as the teletype ticks out the details of the mission, the ops phones will start ringing all over the base, bodies will jerk out of bed, jeeps and trucks will roar as the first preparations are made.

Unseen Army, On Base Striking Arm Of The Eighth. 1944

Introduction

The first steps in the creation of the 3rd Bomb Division began on 12 May 1943 when the 94th, 95th and 96th Bomb Groups in the 1st Bomb Wing in Northamptonshire awaited transfer to Suffolk and Essex to form the nucleus of a new 4th Bomb Wing. All three groups were equipped with B-17F Flying Fortresses with long-range 'Tokyo tanks' built into their wings and the tips to hold an additional 1,080 gallons of fuel. The 94th, 95th and 96th Bomb Groups were to relocate to Earls Colne, Framlingham and Andrews Field respectively. The new organization's first CO was Brigadier General Frederick L. Anderson, whose HQ was at Marks Hall, near Colchester in Essex. The three groups remained in 1st Bomb Wing 'country' until their new bases were completed. The ground echelons of the 94th, 95th and 96th Bomb Groups had only arrived in the United Kingdom on 10 May. On the night of the 12th orders arrived at Bassingbourn, Alconbury and Grafton Underwood respectively, calling for a maximum effort for a mission to St. Omer–Longuenesse airfield in France, starting at 1300 hours. Remarkably, the three new groups managed to put up seventy-two bombers for the mission (which was also flown by the 1st Bomb Wing's newly-arrived 351st Bomb Group) but at such short notice problems were bound to occur. The 96th Bomb Group lost a B-17 when it crashed into The Wash minutes after take-off and the group subsequently failed to bomb the target due to a misunderstanding among the formation leaders. The 351st

Bomb Group formation of fourteen B-17s abandoned the mission in mid-Channel. Thirty-one B-17s in the 94th and 95th Bomb Groups continued to the target but they too were to experience difficulty. Captain Franklin 'Pappy' Colby in the 94th Bomb Group, at 41 years of age the oldest combat pilot in the 8th Air Force, was on the mission.

After many diversions and buzzing around over the North Sea to get the enemy fighters up and, hopefully, low on gas, we finally sallied across the Channel. As the weather was CAVU (Ceiling and Visibility Unlimited) we could see both shores plainly. From our height it looked like we could spit across the Straits of Dover. Major Louis G. Thorup led the High Squadron with me leading the second element of three ships behind him. It turned out to be a piece of cake. We saw no fighters and only three bursts of flak. However, the bombing smelled, as we completely missed the aerodrome and put the bombs out in fields with quite a few going into the town itself. It was a downwind bomb run and apparently our lead bombardier badly underestimated the force of the wind at 20,000ft.

The following day 196 bombers made simultaneous attacks on four targets. Fifteen B-17s in the 96th and 351st Bomb Groups bombed Wevelghem airfield in Belgium and forty-two B-17s in the 94th and 95th Bomb Groups struck at the Ford and General Motors plant and locks in Antwerp. Wevelghem was badly damaged and III/JG26 were forced to move to Lille-Nord. Flak and Fw 190s were evident and a 95th Bomb Group B-17 flown by Lieutenant J. E. McKinley, badly shot up in an earlier fighter attack, spun out of formation from a height of 2,500ft and crashed on the Dutch island of North Beveland, killing the ten-man crew. Altogether, the missions cost the AAF twelve B-17s and B-24s. The bomber gunners and escorting fighters claimed sixty-seven German aircraft shot down. On 19 May 102 B-17s hit Kiel and sixty-four Fortresses bombed Flensburg, while a smaller force flew a diversion. The Flensburg force returned without loss but six Fortresses that attacked Kiel were shot down, three of these being ripped apart by bombs dropped from above them by Fw 190s. On 21 May, ninety-eight B-17s attacked Wilhelmshaven

Contrails produced by fighter escorts and Fortresses dot the sky as the
B-17s head for their target. *(USAF)*

and sixty-three bombed Emden. On the 27th only eleven bombers
hit St. Nazaire. Two days later 147 aircraft returned to the French
port and dropped their bombs on the U-boat pens in what proved
to be the last raid flown by VIII Bomber Command that month.

The 94th Bomb Group moved from Thurleigh to Earls Colne,
in Essex and the 96th Bomb Group was transferred from Grafton
Underwood to Andrews Field, six miles west of Earls Colne.
Finally, the 95th Bomb Group left Alconbury for Framlingham, in
Suffolk, its departure being marred by a tragic accident on 27 May
when a B-17F in the 412th Bomb Squadron exploded while in the
process of being loaded with ten 500lb bombs. Nineteen officers
and men were killed and twenty severely injured, one of whom
later died. Four B-17s parked near the explosion were destroyed
and eleven others damaged.

In June General Ira Eaker, Commanding General of VIII
Bomber Command sent both the 1st and 4th Bomb Wings on two-
pronged attacks against Emden, Kiel, Bremen, Wilhelmshaven
and Cuxhaven in northern Germany on a single day. On the
11th the B-17s set out to bomb Bremen again but the target was
covered with cloud down to about 5,000ft. Cloud also partially
covered Wilhelmshaven. Even so, 168 Fortresses got their bombs
away on target, while thirty others hit the secondary target at

Cuxhaven. About twenty fighters attacked the low groups in the 4th Bomb Wing, which lost one B-17, while sixty-two Fortresses returned with damage and eighty-five fighters were claimed shot down. However, only seven *Luftwaffe* fighters were destroyed or damaged and two pilots were injured. The bomber numbers were still too small but in June the 100th Bomb Group arrived, going first to Podington, then to Thorpe Abbotts, in Suffolk. Two more groups, the 385th commanded by Colonel Elliott Vandevanter and the 388th Bomb Group, which was earmarked for Great Ashfield, would increase the strength of the 4th Bomb Wing to six groups.

On 13 June meanwhile, the 4th Bomb Wing set out for the U-boat yards at Kiel, taking off from their bases at Andrews Field, Earls Colne and Framlingham for the last time. The three Fortress groups were to swap places with three B-26 Marauder groups, which had suffered heavy losses. The move was intended to reduce B-26 mission time so that they could receive better fighter cover. The three 4th Bomb Wing groups would land at the former B-26 bases at Bury St. Edmunds (Rougham) and Horham, in Suffolk and Snetterton Heath, in Norfolk on return from Kiel. Unfortunately, their last mission from their old bases was a disaster. The twin-pronged attack on the coast did not split the German fighter force as hoped and they concentrated on the four combat boxes in the 4th Wing. The Kiel force was attacked before they crossed the enemy coast and just after the bomb run. *Luftwaffe* fighters shot down nine B-17s in the 94th Bomb Group, six of them going down in the combat area. The rest straggled back to Suffolk. The leading 95th Bomb Group formation of seventeen B-17s had at its head, Brigadier General Nathan Bedford Forrest III from HQ 402nd Provisional Combat Bomb Wing riding in the co-pilot's seat of the command aircraft flown by Captain Harry A. Stirwalt. A massive diving frontal attack raked the lead aircraft with cannon fire from one end to the other and Stirwalt's B-17 fell out of formation and spiralled down. All thirteen men aboard baled out, but only the group navigator survived. Forrest was the first American general to be lost in combat in Europe. Four of the six B-17s in the low squadron were shot down also. Two more B-17s in the high squadron and three in the composite group formation took the 95th Bomb Group's total losses to ten. Altogether, the 4th Bomb Wing lost twenty-two B-17s.

Elveden Hall. *(Author)*

General Eaker referred to the Kiel mission as a 'great battle' and he stated that he was satisfied with the results. Brigadier General Anderson, CO 4th Bomb Wing, said, 'It was a privilege to lead such men, who but yesterday were kids in school. They flew their Forts in the face of great opposition like veterans'. The new 4th Bomb Wing CO, Colonel (later Brigadier General) Curtis E. LeMay, who moved into the former HQ of the 3rd Bomb Wing at Elveden Hall, near Thetford, visited the 94th Bomb Group at Rougham. He said that he was going to improve the poor formation flying, which had caused many of the losses and, Colonel John 'Dinty' Moore, CO of the 94th Bomb Group and Colonel Alfred A. Kessler, CO, 95th Bomb Group, were transferred out. Colonel Fred Castle and Colonel John Gerhart respectively, took over. Gerhart had been one of the Eighth's original staff officers at its activation in January 1942, while Castle had accompanied Eaker to England in February of that same year.

General Curtis E. LeMay. *(USAF)*

On 22 June Eaker sent his bombers on the first really deep penetration of Germany, to the chemical and synthetic rubber plant at Hüls, near Recklinghausen. The raid was part of the directive taken by the Allied leaders at the Casablanca Conference in mid-February 1943 called Operation Pointblank, which emphasized the need to reduce the German fighter force. Huls produced approximately 29 per cent of Germany's synthetic rubber and 18 per cent of its total rubber supply. It was also the most heavily defended target in the *Reich* at the time. Most of the route was flown without escort and the mission relied heavily on diversionary feints over the North Sea. Plans went awry when a formation of twenty-one B-17s in the 100th Bomb Group, which should have made its theatre debut, was prevented from taking off because of ground mist and other problems. The 182 B-17s that made it to the target came under repeated attack and sixteen Fortresses were shot down.

On 25 June 275 B-17s were sent to bomb targets in north-west Germany. Cloud hampered bombing at Hamburg, the main objective, and split up the formations, scattering some of the groups and making them an open invitation to fighter attack. Three 4th Bomb Wing B-17s were lost while sixty-one were damaged. Fortress gunners claimed sixty-two fighters shot down, although the real score was twelve lost and six damaged. Cloud interfered in the early evening of the 26th too, when eighty-one 4th Bomb Wing Fortresses bombed Le Mans airfield. Two days later 191 B-17s in the 1st and 4th Bomb Wings (the latter fitted with long-range tanks for the first time) flew to St Nazaire, while fifty bombers headed further inland to Beaumont-le-Roger airfield. German controllers waited until the Spitfire escort had turned back and then sent their fighters up. Nine Fortresses including three in the 95th Bomb Group were shot down and fifty-seven B-17s that attacked St Nazaire returned with battle damage and three dead crewmen aboard.

On 10 July a heavy escort of Spitfires and P-47s accompanied 101 B-17s in the 4th Bomb Wing attacking Le Bourget airfield. None of the B-17s found the target because of cloud and three Fortresses were shot down on the return journey. One week later a record 332 bombers, including B-17s in the 385th and 388th Bomb Groups, which were flying their first missions, set out for Hannover, but the operation was aborted because of bad weather after the bombers had crossed the Dutch coast. Meanwhile, the 385th Bomb Group at Great Ashfield and the 388th Bomb Group at Knettishall were deemed combat ready. The 390th Bomb Group became the sixth and final group to join the 4th Bomb Wing, at Parham, near Framlingham. All three new groups swelled the ranks of the 4th Bomb Wing for an all-out air offensive which would be known as 'Blitz Week', which began on 24 July when 208 B-17s were dispatched to Heroya and Trondheim in Norway. Only one B-17 was lost and sixty-four were damaged. Next day 218 bombers attacked Hamburg, devastated the night before in the great RAF Bomber Command fire raid, and Kiel. The Kiel force lost four Fortresses, while fifty more returned damaged, two of which crashed on landing. Nineteen bombers failed to return. On the 26th ninety-two bombers hit rubber factories around Hannover while fifty-four more raided shipbuilding yards at Hamburg. Twenty-four aircraft were lost, most of them to enemy fighters. The groups were stood down on 27 July but next day just over 300 bombers were dispatched in two forces to bomb German targets. Bad weather however, interfered with the mission and only forty-nine hit the Fieseler aircraft works at Kassel while twenty-eight more bombed the Fw 190 factory at Oschersleben. Twenty-two bombers were lost. On 29 July eighty-one B-17s in the 4th Bomb Wing bombed the Heinkel aircraft factory at Warnemunde and four Fortresses were shot down. Next day 186 B-17s set out for Kassel, which was bombed by 134 of the Fortresses. Altogether, the AAF lost twelve bombers and six fighters. On 31 July VIII Bomber Command announced a three-day stand-down. In a week of sustained operations about 100 aircraft and ninety combat crews (900 men) had been lost.

The Ruhr was bombed on 12 August, when 243 bombers set out unescorted and twenty-five were lost. Three days later more than 300 bombers were dispatched to targets in Holland and France as part of the Starkey deception plan. This was an attempt to make the Germans believe that an invasion of France was imminent; the intention being to relieve pressure on the USSR and halt troop movements to Italy. Strikes against airfields in France and the Low Countries continued on 16 August but a much bigger effort was expected for the 17th, the anniversary mission of the first heavy bombing raid in the European Theatre of Operations (ETO). The enemy fighter strength in the west was on the increase

and so the plan was to attack simultaneously aircraft plants at
Schweinfurt and Regensburg, the latter being the second largest
plant of its kind in Europe after Wiener Neustadt, near Vienna.
An original intention to bomb all three plants on 7 August had
been disrupted by bad weather, so the plan was changed to bomb
each target when the opportunity arose. Production at Regensburg
was estimated at 200 Bf 109s a month, or approximately 25–30 per
cent of Germany's single-engine aircraft output. The destruction
of the Regensburg plant could cause a nine-month delay in
production and *Luftwaffe* operational strength being immediately
affected for up to two months. The 1st Bomb Wing was given
Schweinfurt as their target and Colonel Curtis E. LeMay would
lead the 4th Bomb Wing to Regensburg. To reduce fighter attacks
Le May's B-17s were to fly on to North Africa after bombing
the target while the 1st Bomb Wing flew a parallel course to
Schweinfurt to further confuse the enemy defences and return
to England.

However, the 1st Bomb Wing was delayed by thick inland mist
for 3½ hours after the 4th Bomb Wing had taken off and though
four Thunderbolt groups were to escort the Regensburg force,

Strike photo of Regensburg on 17 August 1943 just after the 390th Bomb
Group had passed over the target. *(USAF)*

only one P-47 group made the rendezvous with the 4th Bomb Wing as planned. They could not possibly protect the long, straggling formation, which stretched for 15 miles and Fortresses in the rear of the formation were left without any protection at all. The enemy fighters began their attacks east of Brussels and in the 1½ hours before the bomb run, seventeen B-17s were shot down. The Bomb Groups were savaged and those that were badly shot-up barely made it over the Alps but the bombing was accurate. Six main workshops at Regensburg were hit and five of them were severely damaged and all production was halted. The attack also destroyed the fuselage jigs for the still secret Me 262 jet fighter. The surviving 128 B-17s, some flying on three engines and many trailing smoke, were attacked by a few fighters on the way to the Alps. LeMay circled his formation over Lake Garda, near Verona, to give the damaged aircraft a chance to rejoin the wing. Red lights were showing on all four fuel-tanks in every bomber and it was a ragged collection of survivors, which finally landed at intervals of up to 50 miles along the North African coast. The 4th Bomb Wing lost twenty-four bombers, with the 100th Bomb Group's nine losses being the largest of all. Altogether, sixty B-17s were missing. This was almost three times the previous highest, when twenty-six bombers were lost on 13 June. A further sixty Fortresses had to be left in Africa for repair. In the final analysis, a staggering 147 Fortresses had been lost while the *Luftwaffe* had lost twenty-seven fighters shot down. Claims by Fortress gunners and P-47 pilot were 288 aircraft destroyed! The almost non-existent maintenance facilities in Africa ruled out any further shuttle missions. LeMay and the 4th Bomb Wing earned the following accolade from Brigadier General Fred Anderson at Wing HQ. 'Congratulations on the completion of an epoch in aerial warfare. I am sure the 4th Bomb Wing has continued to make history. The Hun has no place to hide'.

The B-17s were stood down on 18 August and then on the 19th forty-five Fortresses in the 4th Bomb Wing set out for the airfield at Woensdrecht but none of the Fortresses was able to bomb because of bad weather over the target. One B-17 was lost. The Schweinfurt losses were still having a huge effect on groups and no Fortress missions were flown until 24 August, when the 4th Bomb Wing put up forty-two Fortresses for the raid on airfields again. The B-17s set off again on the 27th when 224

Fortresses escorted by 173 P-47s carried out the first of many raids on V-weapon sites. Some 187 B-17s got their bombs away on Watten. Eight enemy fighters were claimed shot down and four B-17s were lost. Shallow penetration raids remained the order of the day throughout September, as VIII Bomber Command was not yet strong enough to mount raids deep into the Reich. On 2 September airfields in north-western France were bombed. The following morning the 'heavies' pounded Romilly-sur-Seine and other targets in France.

On 13 September VIII Bomber Command was officially divided into three bombardment divisions and the 4th Bomb Wing was renamed the 3rd Bomb Division under the command of Major General Curtis E. LeMay. The 447th Bomb Group had been activated in May 1943 and would become operational on Christmas Eve 1943. The 452nd Bomb Group would join the Division on 5 February 1944. Five more B-24 groups – 486th, 487th, 34th, 490th and 493rd – would join during 1944 to take the total number to fourteen bomb groups by the war's end.

On 15 September 1943 meanwhile, a force of 140 bombers attacked the Renault works and a ball-bearing plants in Paris, while a similar number went for German airfields at Chartres and Romilly-sur-Seine. The following day the 3rd Bomb Division flew a 900-mile, 11-hour round trip to Bordeaux to attack an aircraft plant and returned some of the way in darkness. Before the mission, the crews had practised taking off in squadrons and assembling as a group at night. Just off the southwest coast of England the B-17s encountered heavy rain squalls and these, plus the impending darkness, dispersed the formation. The storm front knocked radio altimeters out of calibration by about 1,000ft and many pilots got into difficulties. Three B-17s ditched in the North Sea and two others crashed. In all, the Eighth lost thirteen bombers. Trials of the British-designed airborne ground-scanning H$_2$S radar were carried out on 23 September and the results proved impressive. On the morning of the 24th crews were alerted for a mission to Stuttgart, but poor weather forced its cancellation. Instead, a practice mission was flown by the 3rd Bomb Division to test new Pathfinder Force (PFF) equipment and techniques, bomb loads being hastily removed and some aircraft stripped of their guns. The Fortresses B-17s completed assembly without incident, but over the North Sea fifteen fighters bounced them.

General Eaker ordered that H_2S-equipped Fortresses should accompany the force of 305 bombers to Emden on 27 September. The German port was chosen because of its proximity to water, which would show up reasonably well on the cathode ray tubes. In all, 244 bombers hit the target and the radar-equipped B-17s performed well. One of the three combat wings in the 3rd Bomb Division managed to bomb visually after exploiting a gap in the clouds, but subsequent photographic reconnaissance proved that only the H_2S-assisted formations had managed to place a fair concentration of bombs on Emden. Other bomb patterns ranged as far as 5 miles from the city. The H_2S sets seemed to provide the answer to the Eighth's accuracy problems and Eaker was anxious to use them again as soon as possible. A period of bad weather gave the technicians time to iron out some of the teething troubles before the bombers returned to Emden on 2 October with two H_2S-equipped aircraft. P-47Ds, fitted with 108-gallon belly tanks, escorted the bombers as far as Duren on 4 October, when 282 bombers attacked Frankfurt, Wiesbaden and Saarbrücken. Twelve B-17s were lost, but without PFF available, cloud ruled out accurate bombing at all primary targets.

Four days later more than 350 bombers attacked Bremen, the 1st and 4th Combat Bomb Wings approaching the target from two different directions to try to fool the German controllers. Airborne Carpet radar jammers aboard some of the B-17s were also used for the first time. The raid proved a disaster for the 100th Bomb Group, which lost seven B-17s. The Eighth lost twenty-six bombers in total, fourteen of them from the 3rd Bomb Division. Next day 378 B-17s bombed targets in East Prussia and Poland on the 3rd Bomb Division's longest mission to date when 115 B-17s headed to the Arado aircraft component plant at Anklam, near Peenemünde. They were a diversion for the 263 Fortresses in the 4th Combat Bomb Wing, which attacked the Polish port of Gdynia (a 1,500-mile round trip), and the Focke-Wulf plant at Marienburg. The Marienburg force achieved the greatest success of the day. The Germans believed anti-aircraft defences to be unnecessary so far from England and their absence meant that the force could bomb from between 11,000 and 13,000ft. At such heights accuracy was almost guaranteed and 60 per cent of the bombs dropped by the ninety-six Fortresses exploded within 1,000ft of the MPI (Mean Point of Impact) and 83 per cent fell within 2,000ft.

Before the raid, the Marienburg plant had been responsible for almost half of the *Luftwaffe's* Fw 190 production. The results were devastating and Eaker called it a classic example of precision bombing. Twenty-eight bombers were lost. Next day, 10 October, when Münster was the target, the unlucky 13th Combat Bomb Wing, comprising the 95th, 100th (low group) and 390th Bomb Groups was savaged by fighter attacks. The 'Bloody Hundredth' formation lost twelve Fortresses, the 390th eight and the 95th Bomb Group, five. Only the arrival of the Thunderbolts prevented further carnage. In all, twenty-nine B-17s were lost by the 3rd Bomb Division and, eighty-eight bombers had been lost on three successive days. The losses came at a time when intelligence sources revealed that German fighter strength was increasing.

No missions were flown between 11 and 13 October but Major General Frederick F Anderson, Commanding General VIII Bomber Command, was biding his time to attack Schweinfurt, which went ahead on 14 October. Anderson hoped to launch 420 Fortresses and Liberators in a three-pronged attack on the city but ultimately, of the 320 B-17s and B-24s sent off, only 229 were effective. Schweinfurt soaked up 482.8 tons of high explosives and incendiaries but the 1st Bomb Division lost forty-five B-17s and the 3rd Bomb Division fifteen. Of these the 96th Bomb Group lost seven, the 94th, six and the 95th and 390th one apiece. The 100th, 385th and 388th Bomb Groups suffered no losses. Of the bombers that returned to England, 142 in both divisions were damaged as a result of fighter attack and flak. Sixty Fortresses and 600 men were missing. Five B-17s had crashed in England because of their battle-damaged condition and twelve more were destroyed in crash landings or were so badly damaged that they had to be written off. Of the returning bombers, 121 required repairs and another five fatal casualties and forty-three wounded crewmen were removed from the aircraft. Claims were for 186 enemy fighters shot down but the actual figure was about thirty-five.

Brigadier General Orvil A. Anderson, Chairman of the Combined Operational Planning Committee, said, 'The entire works are now inactive. It may be possible for the Germans to eventually restore 25 per cent of normal capacity, but even that will require some time'. Air Marshal Sir Charles Portal, Britain's Chief of the Air Staff, added, 'The Schweinfurt raid may well go down in history as one of the decisive air actions of the war and it may

prove to have saved countless lives by depriving the enemy of
a great part of his means of resistance'. However, only eighty-
eight out of the 1,222 bombs dropped actually fell on the plants.
Production at the Kugelfischer plant (largest of the five) was
interrupted for only six weeks. General 'Hap' Arnold confidently
told reporters, 'Now we have got Schweinfurt!'

The losses and a spell of bad weather, restricted VIII Bomber
Command to just two more missions in October. On 3 November
566 B-17s and B-24s headed for Wilhelmshaven when seven
bombers were lost. Two days later 323 B-17s bombed Gelsenkirchen
and 104 B-24s hit Münster. Three B-24s and eight B-17s were lost.
On 11 November the 3rd Bomb Division attacked Münster again.
Mission aborts by the PFF aircraft caused the 95th, 96th, 100th and
388th Bomb Groups to turn back before the enemy coast, leaving
just sixty-one unescorted B-17s in the 94th, 385th and 390th (in the
4th and 13th Combat Bomb Wings) to continue to the target. Four
B-17s were lost. For the first two weeks of November England was
blanketed by thick fog and airfields were lashed with intermittent
showers and high winds. On the 13th 272 B-17s and B-24s were
sent to bomb Bremen, although only 143 bombers got their bombs
away and sixteen heavies were lost. On 16 November VIII Bomber
Command bombed targets in Norway. The 1st Bomb Division
visited the molybdenum mines at Knaben and the 3rd Bomb
Division bombed a generating plant at Vermark in the Rjukan
Valley. Both targets were connected with German heavy water
experiments, which were intended to give the Nazis the atomic
bomb. Five days later the 'heavies' revisited Gelsenkirchen and on
26 November 633 aircraft, the largest formation so far assembled
by VIII Bomber Command, bombed targets as far apart as Bremen
and Paris. Twenty-nine B-17s and five fighters were lost. On the
30th, 381 bombers set out for Solingen in the Ruhr but cloud
prevented accurate bombing and on 1 December 299 bombers
returned to the city. This time the raid was more successful and
281 sorties were effective, although the 3rd Bomb Division was
prevented from bombing because of the weather.

On 30 December the 3rd Bomb Division attacked the IC
Farbenindustrie chemical works at Ludwigshafen. Six Fortresses
in the 100th Bomb Group returned with battle damage and
seventeen B-17s and six B-24s were lost. Next day VIII Bomber

Command mounted all-out raids on airfields in France when twenty-five bombers and four fighters were lost.

On 11 January 1944 291 Fortresses were sent to Oschersleben and Halberstadt. Fighter opposition was the heaviest since the Schweinfurt mission of 14 October the previous year and forty-two Fortresses and two fighters were lost. Ten days later 795 B-17s and B-24s set out to bomb V-weapon sites and other targets in the Pas de Calais and Cherbourg. Some aircraft attacked targets of opportunity, while other combat boxes remained in their areas for too long as they tried to identify targets. A total of 628 fighters escorted the bombers but bombing was restricted by heavy cloud over most of northern France and fewer than half the bombers dropped their bombs accurately. The bombers were stood down for two days but resumed operations on 24 January, when 857 aircraft were sent to bomb aviation industry plants and marshalling yards at Frankfurt. Bad weather during assembly led to a recall, although the leading combat wing in the 3rd Bomb Division, which had reached the German border, decided to bomb a target of opportunity and carried on. Fighter attacks over Belgium claimed two B-17s in the 95th Bomb Group. The weather remained bad and the next bombing mission was not flown until the 29th, when the target was Frankfurt for 863 bombers. In all, twenty-four B-17s and five B-24s were lost.

In February Operation Argument, a series of co-ordinated raids on the German aircraft industry, supported by RAF night bombing finally went ahead, on the 20th and the series of missions soon went into folklore as 'Big Week'. On 20 February 1,028 B-17s and B-24s escorted by 832 fighters attacked twelve aircraft plants in Germany, losing twenty-five bombers and four fighters. Next day 924 bombers escorted by 679 fighters bombed aircraft factories at Brunswick for the loss of nineteen bombers and five fighters. Sixty German fighters were claimed shot down. Bad weather kept the bombers on the ground on the 23rd but on the 24th 238 Fortresses attacked Schweinfurt. Eleven were lost. Meanwhile, 295 B-17s struck targets on the Baltic coast at a cost of five Fortresses. On the 25th the USAAF brought the curtain down on 'Big Week' when 1,300 bombers in the Eighth and Fifteenth Air Forces, escorted by 1,000 fighters, headed for aircraft plants, ball-bearing works and components factories. The 3rd Bomb Division and the Fifteenth Air Force, the latter hitting the targets an hour before the main force arrived from England, heavily damaged the Bf 109 plants at Regensburg. Output at Augsburg and Regensburg was severely reduced for four months. The Eighth lost thirty-one bombers and the Fifteenth, thirty-three. In all, 'Big Week' cost 226 bombers.

On 3 March the USAAF launched its first attack on Berlin but the 748 bombers had to abort because of bad weather and seventy-nine B-17s attacked targets of opportunity in Wilhelmshaven. Next day 502 Fortresses and their fighter escorts set out for 'Big B' until severe weather en route led to a recall and 219 Fortresses bombed targets of opportunity instead. Thirty B-17s in the 95th and 100th Bomb Groups did not get the recall signal and carried on to Berlin alone. Luckily their Mustang escort was still with them and they prevented a massacre when, 14 minutes from the capital, German fighters attacked the bombers. The 95th lost four aircraft and the 100th one but the first US bombs had been dropped on Berlin. The 95th and 100th Bomb Groups were later awarded a Distinguished Unit Citation (DUC). The B-17s were stood down on the 5th while B-24s attacked targets in France. On 6 March the Eighth dispatched 730 B-17s and B-24s accompanied by 801 escort fighters to targets in the suburbs of Berlin. The 3rd Bomb Division which attacked the Robert Bosch Electrical Equipment factory, was hit repeatedly and the unprotected 13th Combat Bomb Wing comprising the 95th, 100th and 390th Bomb Groups, lost twenty-three B-17s or damaged them so badly they were forced to ditch or crash-land on the Continent. In all the 3rd Bomb Division lost thirty-five B-17s, with the 'Bloody Hundredth' losing fifteen of them. Air Marshal Arthur 'Bomber' Harris sent a message on behalf of the RAF to his opposite number, Carl Spaatz, at High Wycombe. 'Heartiest congratulations on the first US bombing of Berlin. It is more than a year since they were attacked in daylight, but now they have no safety there by day or night. All Germany learns the same lesson'.

The Eighth was stood down on 7 March, but the following day more than 600 bombers, escorted by 891 fighters, returned for the third raid on 'Big-B' in a week. The 3rd Bomb Division led the Eighth to the VKF ball-bearing plant at Erkner, in the suburbs east of Berlin, More than 460 bombers hit Erkner with 'good results', while seventy-five others bombed targets of opportunity. The 3rd Bomb Division lost twenty-three Fortresses, sixteen of them in the leading 45th Combat Bomb Wing. Gunners claimed sixty-three fighters, while the escorts claimed seventy-nine for the loss of eighteen of their own but only twenty-seven German fighters were lost. Despite the continued high losses, the Eighth Air Force attacked Berlin again on the 9th with 361 B-17s escorted by 800 fighters. Just six B-17s were lost. Smaller scale raids on targets in France and Germany followed and on 15 March 344 bombers bombed aircraft component factories at Brunswick. Next day, B-17s and B-24s bombed targets in Augsburg, Ulm, Gessertshausen and Friedrichshafen. Gunners claimed sixty-eight enemy fighters. After stand-down on the 17th, the 'heavies' were out again the following day when 738 B-17s and B-24s attacked Oberpfaffenhofen Lechfeld, Landsberg, Memmingen, Munich and Friedrichshafen. Forty-three bombers and thirteen of the 925 fighters that took part were lost. 1944 was invasion year and on 13 April overall command of the Combined Bomber Offensive and the Eighth Air Force officially passed to General Dwight D Eisenhower, newly appointed Supreme Allied Commander. On 29 April 579 bombers bombed the mainline and underground railway system in Berlin and thirty-eight other bombers attacked targets of opportunity. Fw 190s shot down or fatally damaged seventeen Fortresses in the 4th Combat Bomb Wing in just 20 minutes. The 385th Bomb Group, which was flying its 100th mission, lost seven B-l7s and the 447th Bomb Group eleven. The latter's losses brought its monthly total to twenty-one. The 94th and 96th Bomb Groups' losses for April 1944 were also twenty-one bombers each; the Eighth's heaviest of the war.

On 9 May 823 B-17s and B-24s escorted by 668 fighters bombed marshalling yards and airfields in France, Luxembourg and Belgium. Two days later 609 B-17s bombed marshalling yards in Germany and the Low Countries. Eight Fortresses and eight Liberators were lost. On 12 May 886 B-17s and B-24s escorted by 980 fighters carried out the first attack on oil production centres in the Reich when five main plants in central Germany and Czechoslovakia were bombed. Two composite 4th Combat Bomb Wing formations battled their way through 200 plus enemy fighters to attack an Fw 190 depot at Zwickau. Eleven bombers, including seven in the 447th Bomb Group, were shot down. The Fortresses, which fought their way through to the target at Zwickau, achieved a highly effective bomb pattern. The 385th Bomb Group, led by Colonel Elliott Vandevanter placed 97 per cent of its bombs within 2,000ft of the MPI to earn the group a DUC. In what was one of the fiercest air battles of the war, thirty bombers in the 3rd Bomb Division were shot down. Worst hit was the 45th Combat Bomb Wing, the 452nd Bomb Group losing fourteen B-17s, the 96th twelve and the 388th one. On 13 May 749 bombers attacked oil refineries at Politz on the Baltic coast and the marshalling yards at Osnabrück. Twelve B-17s and B-24s were lost. The fighter escorts claimed forty-seven enemy fighters shot down for the loss of five of their own. Two day's later 166 B-17s and B-24s bombed V-weapon sites in France. No bombers were lost and 128 bombers dropped 485 tons of HE on the 'Noball' (V-1) sites. On 19 May 888 B-17s and B-24s were dispatched, 588 Fortresses attacking targets in Berlin and Kiel while 300 Liberators went to Brunswick. Fighter opposition was heavy and twenty-eight bombers were lost. US fighters claimed seventy enemy aircraft for the loss of nineteen of their own. On the 20th 271 B-24s and B-17s in the 3rd Bomb Division set out to bomb Liege and Brussels but heavy cloud resulted in the 3rd Bomb Division having to abandon the mission. The bombers returned to France the next day and on the 22nd they bombed Kiel and Siracourt. Five B-17s were lost. With good weather continuing, the bombers made visual bombing attacks on targets in France on 23, 24 and 25 May. On the 27th the Eighth switched to German targets and 24 bombers were lost. On 28 May 1,341 bombers hit oil targets in Germany and thirty-two bombers were lost. Next day 888 B-24s and B-17s made visual bombing attacks on aircraft plants and oil installations in Germany. Seventeen B-17s were lost and seventeen B-24s also failed to return. The Leuna works suffered a 50 per cent drop in production after the raids in May and the Pölitz works was even worse hit on the 29th. Attacks on the German aircraft industry and marshalling yards in France and Belgium continued on 30 May when 928 bombers in six forces escorted by 672 fighters were out in force. Twelve bombers and nine fighters were lost. Next day 1,029 B-17s and B-24s were dispatched and raids only one bomber and three fighters were lost.

On 6 June – D-Day – a total of 2,362 bomber sorties, involving 1,729 B-17s and B-24s, were flown and 3,596 tons of bombs were dropped for the loss of just three Liberators. Ground crews worked through the night of 5/6 June to ensure that numerous sorties could be flown on D-Day. On the 8th 1,135 bombers attacked communication targets in France. Bad weather prevented 400 bombers from hitting their targets and the following day it ruled out any strikes altogether and also severely curtailed operations on 10 June. Of the 873 bombers dispatched, more than 200 were forced to abort because of cloud but 589 bombers, including thirty-one Pathfinders, attacked eight airfields in France and nine coastal installations in the Pas de Calais. On 11 and 12 June bad weather ruled out targets in Germany and so the bombers went to France again. Tactical targets were attacked until the 15th, when 1,225 bombers bombed an oil refinery at Misburg. On 20 June oil targets were hit again for the loss of twelve B-17s and thirty-seven B-24s and twelve fighters. On 21 June the Eighth flew its second shuttle mission when 1,311 B-17s set off for Berlin in Operation Frantic. Sixty-three B-17s in the 13th and 45th Combat Bomb Wings attacked the Ruhrland-Elsterwerda synthetic oil plant 50 miles south of Berlin, escorted by seventy P-51s in the 4th and 352nd Fighter Groups, before flying to airfields in the Soviet Union. (A second formation, made up of the rest of the 3rd Bomb Division, the 1st Bomb Division and the 2nd Bomb Division, bombed Berlin and returned to England). Near Cuxhaven four B-17s in the 452nd Bomb Group were involved in a mid-air collision. The shuttle force touched down at Poltava, where a few hours later sixty *Luftwaffe* bombers destroyed forty-four of the seventy-two bombers and severely damaged twenty-six others. Further losses were avoided by the 13th Combat Bomb Wing at Mirgorod and by the Mustangs at Piryatin, when they flew 150 miles further east to safety. General Spaatz conceded later that the Poltava raid was the 'best attack the *Luftwaffe* ever made on the AAF'.

Late in July the ball turrets were removed from many Liberators to improve stability and altitude performance. During the last week of July General Doolittle carried out the first stage of his plan to convert all Liberator groups in England to Fortresses. The 486th Bomb Group at Sudbury and the 487th Bomb Group at Lavenham, which formed the 92nd Wing, were taken off operations and by the end of the month, were ready to begin combat missions in Fortresses. Between the end of August and mid-September the three B-24 groups in the 93rd Wing (the 34th, 490th and 493rd), also changed over to the B-17G. On 1 August the 486th and 487th

Bomb Groups flew their first B-17 mission. The 95th Wing, which had begun with only two groups, ceased to exist on 14 August, when the 489th was transferred to the 20th Wing as a fourth group. On 27 August the 490th Bomb Group flew their first B-17G mission. On 8 September it was the turn of the 493rd Bomb Group at Debach. Finally, on 17 September the 34th Bomb Group switched to the B-17G. At first crews resented the changeover but they quickly grew to like the improved flying characteristics inherent in the B-17 and they praised the more spacious nose compartment and improved heating. However, changing over to the Fortress was practically a guarantee that from now on the former B-24 groups would be visiting 'Big League' targets like Bremen, Merseburg, Magdeburg, Ludwigshafen, Münster and other German cities, which was quite different from bombing V-1 launching sites in France.

In August the Fortresses bombed airfields in France and strategic targets in Germany. On the first day of the month 191 B-17s dropped supplies to the French Resistance. On the 4th the bombers returned to strategic targets, when 1,250 'heavies' hit oil refineries, aircraft factories, airfields and the experimental establishment at Peenemünde in two separate raids. On the 5th 1,062 bombers attacked eleven oil-producing plants in central Germany, without loss. Next day 953 bombers raided Berlin and oil and manufacturing centres in the Reich for the loss of twenty-five bombers, and seventy-five Fortresses in the 95th and 390th Bomb Groups bombed the Focke-Wulf plant at Rahmel in Poland. After the raid the two groups flew on to their shuttle base at Mirgorod, in the USSR, the scene of such devastation two months before. While there the 95th and 390th Bomb Groups mounted a raid on the Trzebina synthetic oil refinery, before flying to Italy on 8 August, bombing two Romanian airfields en route. Four days later they flew back to East Anglia on the last stage of their shuttle, bombing Toulouse-Franycaal airfield as they crossed France. This third long-ranging operation had proven more successful than the disastrous one in June and not a single B-17 was lost.

In England, meanwhile, bad weather throughout September severely limited missions and only fourteen were flown during the entire month. On 12 September 217 B-17s in the 3rd Bomb Division attacked the Brabag synthetic oil refinery, Rothensee and the ordnance depot at Friedrichstadt in Magdeburg, which was heavily defended by flak batteries armed with 88mm and 105mm guns. About 450 fighters attacked the 3rd Bomb Division formations and forty-five aircraft were shot down. The raid on Magdeburg alone cost the 493rd Bomb Group twelve Fortresses.

In mid-September the B-17s flew a mercy drop to the beleaguered Polish Home Army in the ruins of Warsaw. The Polish capital was totally cut off from the outside world, with the German army on one side and the Soviets on the other. Stalin had asked Polish General Bor to rise against the German occupiers, but had then stood by while the gallant Poles were gradually annihilated. It was not until early September that the Soviet leader finally agreed to co-operate by allowing the B-l7s to fly on to the USSR after the supply drops. An attempt to reach Warsaw on 15 September was aborted because of bad weather and it was not until the 18th that the 13th Combat Bomb Wing was able to fly all the way. Colonel Karl Truesdell Jr, 95th Bomb Group CO, led the B-17s over Warsaw and the supply drop was made from between 13,000ft and 18,000ft, amid limited but accurate flak. The strong American fighter escort was unable to prevent the *Luftwaffe* attacking the 390th Bomb Group, which was flying as the low group, during the dropping run. One Fortress was shot down and another landed at Brest–Litovsk. However, the remaining aircraft succeeded in reaching their shuttle bases at Mirgorod and Poltava. On 19 September they took off again for the now-familiar return flight via Italy and France, but this time without bombing any targets en route because all French territory had now been liberated.

On 27 September the B-17s bombed oil targets and engineering centres in Cologne, Ludwigshafen and Mainz. Magdeburg, Kassel and Merseburg were attacked a day later, for the loss of thirty bombers. Eight days later, on 6 October, the 385th Bomb Group lost eleven B-17s when the Eighth returned to Berlin. Only the arrival of the P-51 escort prevented further carnage. Despite mounting losses, there was increasing evidence that the Eighth's bombing offensive, particularly against oil targets, was reaping rewards and Doolittle continued to apply pressure on Germany's oil manufacturing industry. On 7 October more than 1,300 B-17s and B-24s bombed five synthetic oil plants for the loss of fifty-two bombers. On 14 October 1,100 B-17s and B-24s bombed marshalling yards and targets in the Cologne area. Bad weather throughout November slowed down the Allies' advance all along the western front and severely hampered missions. When flown, they were usually against oil targets, as on 2 November when 1,100 bombers attacked four large German synthetic oil refineries including the I G Farbenindustrie refinery at Leuna, three miles south of Merseburg, which was defended by an estimated 500 fighters. Altogether, the Eighth lost forty bombers and twenty-eight fighters. It was for his actions that 2nd Lieutenant Robert E. Femoyer, a navigator in the 447th Bomb Group, was posthumously awarded the Medal of Honor. The losses were so bad that groups were stood down for 48 hours after the raid and then, on 5 November, a mission to Ludwigshafen went ahead. On 9 November tactical missions were flown in support of General George Patton's 3rd Army, which was halted at Metz and German lines of communication at Saarbrücken, as well as enemy gun emplacements to the east and south of Metz, were bombed, to enable the advance through Belgium to continue. The mission was given top priority and at bases throughout East Anglia Fortresses taxied out in the mist and bad visibility. The conditions contributed to the loss of eight bombers in take-off and landing accidents and further disasters befell some groups as the mission progressed. Lieutenant's Donald J. Gott and William E. Metzger in the 452nd Bomb Group were awarded posthumous Medals of Honor.

On 16 November aerial support was provided for the advancing US and British armies. The mission was meticulously planned to avoid bombing friendly troops near the targets, just east of Aachen. The Allied artillery fired smoke shells every 500 yards along the front and barrage balloons were placed along the edge of the area. The use of radio signals was especially worth-while when cloud covered the front lines and it helped to ensure accurate bombing. Worsening weather forced some groups to fly to the north of Britain to escape it and they were unable to get back to their bases for a few days. On 21 November the Eighth returned to Merseburg for the first of three more raids on the refineries in a week. On 30 November when 1,200 B-17s and B-24s bombed four synthetic oil refineries in Germany, the 3rd Bomb Division attacked Merseburg. The Eighth Air Force lost twenty-nine heavy bombers but by the end of November more than forty-three refineries, processing both crude and synthetic oil, had been destroyed.

December 1944 brought the worst winter weather in England for 54 years. On the 16th, using appalling conditions to his advantage, Field Marshal Karl von Rundstedt and his Panzer force, supported by an estimated 1,400 fighters, attacked US positions in the forests of the Ardennes on the French-Belgian border and opened up a salient, or 'bulge', in the Allied lines. In England all aircraft were grounded by fog and it was not until the 23rd that they could offer support in the 'Battle of the Bulge'. On Christmas Eve a record 2,034 Eighth Air Force bombers, as well as 500 from the RAF and Ninth Air Force, took part in the largest single strike flown by the Allied air forces in World War 2. Their targets were German airfields and lines of communication leading to the 'Bulge'. Brigadier General Fred Castle, CO of the 4th Combat Bomb Wing who led the 3rd Bomb Division was shot down and was posthumously awarded the Medal of Honor, making him the highest ranking officer in the Eighth Air Force to receive America's supreme military decoration. Overall, the Christmas Eve raids were effective and they severely hampered von Rundstedt's communication links. The cost in aircraft, however, was high. Many crashed on their return over England as drizzle and overcast weather played havoc with landing patterns. Tired crews put down where they could. Only 150 aircraft were available for another strike on 26 December. The following day the wintry conditions were responsible for a succession of crashes during early morning take-offs. On 30 December the Eighth again attacked German communications. On New Year's Eve the 3rd Bomb Divison crews returned to oil production centres. Hamburg was the scene of another disaster for the 100th Bomb Group, which lost twelve B-17s to fighters and flak.

January 1945 marked the start of the Eighth's fourth year of operations and it seemed as if the end of the war was in sight. On the 1st the Bomb Divisions were renamed Air Divisions and the following day the B-I7s once again pounded communication lines. Raids like this went on for several days until the tactical position in the Ardennes gradually swung back in the Allies' favour. On 3 January the severe wintry weather over England was responsible for several fatal accidents during take-off for the mission to Frankfurt. However, a period of fine weather, beginning on the

6th, once again allowed the bombers to fly missions in support of troops on the ground. These were mostly against lines of communication, airfields and marshalling yards. Finally, the German advance in the Ardennes came to a halt and ultimately petered out. Hitler's last chance now lay in his so-called 'wonder weapons': the V1 flying bomb and V2 rocket. Missions were flown to tactical targets throughout the remainder of January, but when the weather intervened, the Eighth mounted shallow penetration raids on 'No Ball' targets in France. By 3 February Marshal Zhukov's Red Army was only 35 miles from Berlin and the capital was jammed with refugees fleeing from the advancing Soviets. Accompanied by 900 fighters, 1,200 B-17s and B-24s dropped 2,267 tons of bombs on the centre of Berlin, killing an estimated 25,000 inhabitants, destroying 360 industrial targets and heavily damaging another 170. Reconnaissance showed that an area 1½-miles square had been devastated. Twenty-one bombers were shot down and six crash-landed inside Soviet lines. Of the bombers that returned, ninety-three had suffered varying degrees of flak damage. Further German disruption in the face of the Soviet advance occurred on 6 February when 1,300 bombers, escorted by fifteen groups of Mustangs, bombed Chemnitz and Magdeburg and synthetic oil refineries at Lutzkendorf and Merseburg. The 490th Bomb Group lost four Fortresses, three of them in mid-air collisions.

On 9 February the 'heavies' returned to the oil refineries in the ever-diminishing Reich, which was now seriously threatened by the Soviet armies converging from the east. The old city of Dresden in eastern Germany was bombed by 800 aircraft of RAF Bomber Command on the night of 13 February and the next day, 400 US bombers attempted to stoke up the fires, while a further 900 attacked Chemnitz, Magdeburg and other targets. On 15 February more than 1,000 bombers hit the Magdeburg synthetic oil plant again. Next day B-17s and B-24s bombed oil targets in Salzbergen, Gelsenkirchen and Dortmund. Bombing was completed visually and the *Luftwaffe* was noticeable by its virtual absence. However, bomber losses continued, mainly as a result of the bad weather, which affected assembly operations over England, and because of flak. On 22 February in Operation Clarion more than 6,000 Allied aircraft from seven different commands bombed transportation targets in western Germany and northern Holland. All targets were selected with the object of preventing troops being transported to the Russian front, now only a few miles from Berlin. Despite the low altitudes flown, only seven bombers were lost.

By March 1945 the systematic destruction of German oil production plants, airfields and communication centres had virtually driven the *Luftwaffe* from German skies. On 15 March 1,353 bombers, escorted by 833 fighters, bombed the German Army HQ at Zossen, near Berlin and a marshalling yard at Oranienburg. Two days later 1,328 B-17s and B-24s, escorted by 820 fighters, bombed targets in west and north central Germany. On 18 March the bombers returned to Berlin. Twelve B-17s and a B-24 were shot down by Me 262s. On 22 March 1,301 B-17s and B-24s bombed targets east of Frankfurt and military encampments in the Ruhr in preparation for the Allied amphibious crossing of the lower Rhine. The Eighth also bombed the Bottrop military barracks and areas directly behind the German lines, while 136 B-17s of the Fifteenth Air Force attacked Ruhrland yet again, causing extensive damage to the industrial complex. Twenty-seven Me 262s attacked the bomber formations and claimed thirteen B-l7s shot down, but only one Fortress was actually lost. Next day 1,244 bombers hit rail targets in the Ruhr. On 23–24 March, under a 66-mile-long smoke screen and aided by 1,749 bombers of the Eighth Air Force, Field Marshal Bernard Montgomery's 21st Army Group crossed the Rhine in the north, while simultaneous crossings were made by General Patton's Third Army further south. Groups flew two missions on 24 March, hitting a number of jet bases in Holland and Germany, while 240 B-24s, each loaded with 600 tons of food, medicines and weapons, dropped vital supplies to the armies in the field.

Finally, on 16 April General Spaatz announced an end to the strategic mission of the Eighth Air Force and only some tactical missions now remained. The following day Dresden was bombed by almost 1,000 aircraft. Eight B-17s and seventeen fighters were shot down, including six B-17s by Me 262s. During the week of 18 to 25 April, missions were briefed and scrubbed almost simultaneously as the ground forces overran objective after objective. The German corridor was shrinking rapidly and the American and Soviet bomb lines now crossed at several points on briefing maps. During the first week of May the German

Third Air Division B-17s lined up on the Continent at the end of the war during repatriation missions. *(TAMM)*

armies surrendered one by one to Montgomery at Luneberg Heath, to Devers at Munich, to Alexander at Casserta and finally to Eisenhower at Rheims in the early hours of 7 May. Starting on 1 May, before the Germans surrendered, Fortress crews flew food mercy missions, called Chowhound, to starving civilians in Holland (together with RAF Manna operations, which had begun on 29 April) until the end of hostilities. The sixth and final Eighth Air Force Chowhound mission was flown on 7 May 1945 – the day before VE-Day – when thirty-nine B-17s in the 493rd Bomb Group dropped their last consignment of British rations over the airfield at Schiphol. This group had played a major role in Chowhound, with thirty-eight B-17s dropping 3,414 cases of food on Rotterdam on 1 May and a further forty bombers (led by group CO Colonel Robert Landry) resupplying Haarlem with 3,510 cases 24 hours later. Robert 'Gus' Gaustad, navigator in Lieutenant Munday's crew at Debach, remembers that on VE-Day, 'in front of a neat and flower-bordered farmhouse not overly far from my hut, a small American flag was displayed, along with a large sign which read, "Thank You America!" I was moved to tears'.

The Airfields

Bury St Edmunds (Rougham) – Station 468

T wo miles east of Bury St. Edmunds and sandwiched between the old A45 (now A14) and Bury–Thurston roads, Rougham airfield was typical of the USAAF bases in the area, being constructed mainly by Richard Costain Ltd to the standard Class 'A' pattern with three intersecting runways, thirty hardstandings and two T2 hangars. The base was handed over to the Eighth Air Force in the autumn of 1942, although then not fully completed. The 47th Bomb Group (Light) with A-20B medium bombers first used the field during September-October 1942 but moved out to Horham after a month and thence to North Africa as part of the 12th Air Force. The first unit to fly operations from Rougham was the 322nd Bomb Group (Medium) equipped with B-26B Marauders, arriving in December 1942. The 322nd Group's first mission was not flown until 14 May 1943 when a Dutch power station near Ijmuiden was the target. Due to poor bombing, the Group was assigned the same target along with another at Haarlem on 17 May. This low-level strike turned out to be a total disaster when the entire force of ten aircraft to reach Holland was lost to enemy action and collisions. About that time a rumour was going around concerning a young blonde lady spy who was said to have had a hand in this tragedy, but this has never been substantiated. To add to the despondency at Rougham a B-26 crashed into a hangar there on 29 May. As a result of the losses sustained on unescorted low-level missions it was decided by HQ Eighth Air Force to switch to medium altitude bombing and from then on the B-26 groups' fortunes improved. A further decision was made to redeploy the 322nd Bomb Group to Andrews Field, Essex, in exchange for a heavy bomb group and the 322nd was subsequently assigned to the Ninth Air Force. One of the Rougham-based Marauders, *Flak Bait*, survived the war and is now an exhibit at the Smithsonian Museum in Washington DC.

The B-17Fs of the 94th Bomb Group first flew into Rougham on Sunday 13 June 1943 following a tough mission to Kiel during which they lost nine aircraft. The 94th had previously been stationed at Earls Colne, Essex, and while the Forts were out attacking Kiel, the ground personnel moved in with all essential equipment. This group, comprising the 331st, 332nd, 333rd and 410th Bomb Squadrons, was part of 4th Combat Bombardment Wing, 3rd Bomb Division. They flew B-17F and later the chin-turreted G versions and carried the code letter A in a black square

B-17F-35-DL 42-3190, 331st Bomb Squadron, which pilot Captain Kee Harrison crash-landed in a French wheat field with its bomb load intact after being shot up on the Paris-Le Bourget mission on 14 July 1943. Harrison and three others evaded and later returned safely to England. Four others were taken prisoner. *(via Zdenek Hurt)*

B-17F-35-DL 42-3190, 332nd Bomb Squadron, shot down by
Oberstleutnant Egon Mayer *Kommandeur*, III./JG 2 on 14 July 1943.
(Harry Holmes)

on the fin. A month after arriving at Rougham, a new Commanding Officer, Colonel Frederick W. Castle, was appointed to succeed
Colonel Moore. At first this change was resented by the crews,
but Colonel Castle soon gained the respect of the Group, which
he led until April 1944, during which time he welded the 94th into
one of the most efficient of the Eighth Air Force.

Rougham offered good Rest & Recuperation (R&R) prospects
for the 94th Bomb Group, with a day at the races at Newmarket
available on occasion and Thetford, birthplace of Thomas Paine, a
radical 18th Century thinker and political writer. He was born
in White Hart Street, Thetford in 1737. He was educated at the
Grammar School in Bridge Street and then moved to London in
1737, writing a series of books and leaflets advocating social and
political change. Paine played a prominent part in the French
and American revolutions and became the unofficial American
Ambassador in 1787, publishing *The Rights of Man* in 1791. He was
accused of sedition and left England never to return. His works
were banned and his effigy burned in many towns. A statue of
Thomas Paine now stands outside the Kings House in Thetford
and there is a permanent display in the Ancient House Museum.
(A B-17 in the 388th Bomb Group at Knettishall bore Thomas
Paine's name). Also, Culford Hall, six miles from Bury St. Edmunds
was built by the Marquis of Cornwallis whose surrender at
Yorktown in 1781 had meant victory for the Americans in the War
of Independence. On the base there was other entertainment. An
American concert party gave a show on 29 June 1943. Star of

B-17F-65-BO 42-29670 *Thundermug*, formerly in the 333rd Bomb Squadron, was transferred to the 544th Bomb Squadron, 384th Bomb Group. It was one of seven in the Group that were lost on 25 July 1943 when it crashed at Hamburg. Two of Lieutenant Kelmer J. Hall's crew were KIA while eight were taken prisoner. *(Richards)*

B-17F-25-DL 42-3088 was assigned to the 410th Bomb Squadron at Rougham in January 1943 and was transferred to the 544th Bomb Squadron, 384th Bomb Group on 12 July. *Sugar Puss* was one of seven 384th Bomb Group B-17s lost on the mission to Hamburg on Sunday 25 July 1943. Six of the losses were from the 544th Bomb Squadron. Four of Lieutenant Clarence R. Cristman's crew were KIA and six survived to be taken prisoner. *(USAF)*

the show was Bob Hope, supported by female vocalist Frances Langford, comedian Jerry Colonna (of the high-pitched voice and rolling eyes) and Jack Pepper.

Targets attacked during 1943 included Wilhelmshaven, Stuttgart, Emden, a number of French targets, the famous shuttle raid on the ball-bearing plant at Regensburg when they flew on to North Africa and for which they were awarded a Distinguished Unit Citation, and the notorious raid on Schweinfurt on 14 October. 2nd Lieutenant Roy G. Davidson, one of the pilots in the 333rd Bomb Squadron recalls:

When the covers were withdrawn on the route map, it showed that the fighter escort only went a short way with us to the target. We would have a long way from France onwards without fighter cover and on the way back too. We knew that we were in for a pretty rough time but we had no idea just how rough it was going to be. We had not been on the first Schweinfurt raid and didn't realize how bad Schweinfurt was. Despite this I really looked forward to the mission because I thought the accomplishment would be great. It never crossed the minds of the crew that we would not complete our twenty-five missions. A telegram was read out telling us that this was one of the most important missions of the war. When we had knocked out the ball-bearing plants the war would come to a halt. We felt we were really going to contribute a lot towards winning the war. I was flying in the low squadron as last man – the most vulnerable spot in the entire formation. But we felt safe because even though we were the last aircraft in a string of over 200 bombers, there were going to be a whole lot of Liberators following right behind us. This would really put us right in the middle of the whole string, which seemed to be a pretty good spot to be in.

My position in the group formation as 'tail-end Charlie' really put us in the centre of the whole shooting match. We went into the target amid very heavy flak and fighter attacks. The fighters continued to attack us right through to the target area. They even flew through their own flak with no let up at all. But we were able to fight them off all the way to the target and out. Carl F. 'Hoot' Gibson, ball turret gunner, shot down a Bf 109 and the boys were really excited about this. But pretty soon the fighters came in thick and fast and everyone was getting to do a lot of shooting. By the time the fight was over I think most of the gunners aboard were out of ammunition. Fred Krueger, in the top turret, ran out and never did get to reload. We went into the target, dropped our bombs and had started back out, when the fighters made passes through the middle of the formation. We outfought the fighters but a Bf 110 pulled in close and fired rockets at us. One of the missiles exploded right under our plane. It felt as if we were on an elevator; it lifted us up and did all kinds of damage. It wasn't long before we had a Bf 109 off each wing about 50 yards out. We had no ammunition left and anyway, three men had baled out and the rear gunner was wounded. They took it in turns to shoot at us, turning in directly from 3 o'clock.

Eventually, Davidson's third engine cut out and he was forced to make a wheels-up landing in a cow pasture near the village

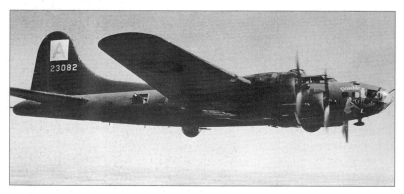

B-17F-25-DL 42-3082 *Double Trouble* in the 333rd Bomb Squadron. The pilot, Lieutenant Bill Winnesheik, aborted the mission to Bremen on 25 June 1943 after fighters knocked out two engines and he landed in England despite a full bomb load. On 4 October 1943, during a mission to St. Dizier, France, fighters knocked out the No. 3 engine and the propeller refused to feather but the crew managed to crash-land at Margate. Vance Van Hooser the assistant engineer/waist gunner, who was on his 23rd mission, was hit in the head by 20mm shell fragments and never flew again. *(USAF)*

B-17F-50-DL 42-3352 *Virgin's Delight* in the 410th Bomb Squadron.
Virgin's Delight and 2nd Lieutenant Walter Chyle's crew FTR on
29 November 1943 when the aircraft was ditched in the North Sea
with the loss of all the crew. *(USAF)*

B-17F-95-BO 42-30248 was
assigned to the 410th
Bomb Squadron, on 2 June
1943 and was named *The
Southern Queen*. In August
this aircraft joined the
333rd Bomb Squadron and
it was renamed *The
Buzzard*, later becoming
The Prodigal Son before
finally becoming *Lassie
Come Home*. 42-30248 and
Lieutenant Robert
C. Randall's crew FTR
from the mission to
Brunswick on 11 January
1944. Two of the crew were
killed and eight survived
to be taken prisoner.
(USAF via Geoff Ward)

1st Lieutenant William F. Cely, pilot and 2nd Lieutenant Jabez
I. Churchill, co-pilot in the 333rd Bomb Squadron, inspect their badly
damaged B-17G-1-VE 42-39775/K *Frenesi*. They brought the B-17 home to
Rougham from Brunswick on 11 January 1944 with three wounded
gunners after five crew and a cameraman had baled out over enemy
territory. Cely added the Silver Star to his DFC and Air Medal for
bringing *Frenesi* back. The aircraft was so badly damaged that it was
scrapped, but five of the crew fought another day in *Frenesi II* (43-38834).
(via Ian McLachlan)

of La Chappele-sur-Orbais. Davidson's crew was one of six 94th
Bomb Group crews lost.

One of the 94th's characters was Captain Franklin 'Pappy'
Colby who at the age of 42 in September 1943 was the oldest
combat pilot in the Eighth Air Force. He was awarded the Air
Medal, the first to be gained by the 94th Group, On 1 April 1943.
At the end of June he was promoted to Major and given command
of the 410th Bomb Squadron. 'Pappy' Colby completed his tour of
twenty-three missions on 30 November 1943.

Another DUC was awarded to the 94th Bomb Group for their
part in the attack on Brunswick on 11 January 1944 when over
570 B-17s and B-24s bombed industrial targets at Oschersleben,
Halberstadt and near Brunswick. It was reported that fighter
opposition was the heaviest since the Schweinfurt mission the

previous October. Andy J. Coroles, a bombardier in the 331st Squadron, 94th Bomb Group, flew the mission to Brunswick:

This was the deepest penetration this group had made into Germany unescorted since Schweinfurt. Our group was heavily hit by Me 110s and Fw 190s and lost eight ships and crews. Our squadron lost three crews: Butler, Rubin and Service. The weather over England was very bad when we took off and assembled. The mission was recalled about the time we left the English coast but Lieutenant Colonel Louis G. Thorup did not receive the message. As a result, our Wing and two others that did not receive the message apparently went on into the target, not knowing the mission had been scrubbed and the fighter escorts recalled. It was a costly mix-up and cost us several good crews.

The weather began clearing up as soon as we reached Germany and was perfectly clear in the area of the target. We made a 'dry run' and had to do a 360-degree turn and come in again. As we started our second bomb run the Me 110s began attacking us. The other two groups in our Wing had dropped their bombs on the first run and headed for home, leaving our group alone. We had a running battle for about an hour; the Me 110s attacking from 3 o'clock around to 9 o'clock with rockets and 20mms. One by one the ships around us would be knocked out of formation. The enemy fighters would then 'gang up' on these cripples and finish them off. Bloyd and Cox were doing violent evasive action all through these attacks and again and again I saw clouds of 20mm shells explode where we had been only a second before. It looked as if our group was going to be picked off one at a time. I was expecting our turn to come at any moment.

About 90 miles from the coast, six P-47s suddenly appeared and scared away the Jerries. Our formation was a sad sight; only ten planes were left out of the original twenty-one. Besides the eight ships from our group that went down, our formation lost three from the 447th Group, which had tacked on to us. I saw one of the 447th ships go down. It was an all silver B-17 carrying the CO of that group. The entire tail of this ship from the waist back was blazing fiercely and one

Me 110 was sitting on his tail not more than 200 yards out, slugging it out with the tail gunner. The tail gunner finally hit the Me 110 and it peeled off and started down smoking heavily. I watched the flames eat their way forward on the ship as it flew on in formation for one or two minutes. Then it suddenly nosed up, fell off on its back and went straight down. No 'chutes came out of it. It was a fascinating sight and one I'll never forget. Our ship came through the entire battle with one small flak hole. The Lord must have been watching over us and I'm thankful to be back from that raid in one piece.

That year saw the Group taking part in 'Big Week' in February, Operation Crossbow (V-weapons sites), softening-up attacks on French targets prior to the Normandy landings with three missions on D-Day, about a dozen visits to 'Big B' (Berlin) in addition to the large number of industrial targets in Germany.

Colonel Charles B. Dougher succeeded Colonel Castle in April 1944 and remained CO until March 1945.

On 13 April 1944 Lieutenant Abe Dolim, a Hawaiian B-17 navigator who, three years before had witnessed at first hand the Japanese bombing of Pearl Harbor, was one of the officers in Joe Hamil's crew that arrived in Scotland aboard the *Queen Elizabeth* on 6 April. On the 11th they arrived at Rougham. Two days later

Dolim was standing outside the ablutions building with another young officer who had graduated from the same navigation class in California and who he had not met since phase training days. Dolim asked his friend about combat flying. The short, intense, dark-haired young man told him about the many losses of personnel, some of

Lieutenant Abe Dolim, a Hawaiian born radio operator who flew two tours in the 94th Bomb Group at Bury St. Edmunds (Rougham). *(Dolim)*

them mutual friends, about the deep penetrations into enemy territory, heavy flak concentrations and fierce fighter attacks. As he spoke, his face revealed a deep down dread and fear of what tomorrow will bring. Dolim was aghast at what he saw and heard and a thought flashed through his mind: 'This man expects to die'. Five days later, on Tuesday, 18 April the 94th Bomb Group experienced the heaviest losses in months of combat. Ten of the crews failed to return from the mission to Berlin and the intense young man was one of those listed as killed in action. Captain Lundak brought his B-17 back 'shot to hell' and minus his tail gunner who had baled out when the pilot dived to the deck from 25,000ft. The crew had used up almost all their ammunition and they could not maintain position with the group. Lieutenant Pearl, Lundak's navigator, told Dolim that they were caught outside the bomber stream by about sixty Fw 190s. Bob Giles and

A stick of 1,000lb bombs dropped from Lieutenant John Winslett's B-17G-30-VE 42-97791 *Trudy*, 332nd Bomb Squadron, over Berlin on 19 May 1944 knocked off the left horizontal stabilizer of Lieutenant Marion Ulysses Reid's B-17G-20-BO 42-31540 *Miss Donna Mae*, 331st Bomb Squadron, below. Reid's aircraft went into an uncontrollable spin and at 13,000ft the wing broke off and the B-17 spun crazily to the ground. There were no survivors. *(USAF via Abe Dolim)*

Norman McComb were Missing in Action (MIA). By the time Dolim flew his first mission (on 22 April) the 94th would have lost about fourteen crews in combat or rotated home.

Glenn Miller and his famous orchestra, with vocalist Dinah Shore visited Rougham on 13 September 1944 on the occasion of the 200th mission celebration party. This really helped things go with a swing. Guest of honour at the event was Brigadier General Castle who by now had been given command of the 4th Combat Wing. General Castle was to lose his life after being shot down on 24 December 1944 while leading a big 3rd Bomb Division attack in the Liege area, For his great gallantry he was posthumously awarded the Medal of Honor – America's highest award.

Returning from the mission to Lutzkendorf, Germany on 30 November 1944 B-17Gs 42-97985 and 44-8177 were involved in a mid-air collision at Battles Corner, Rougham killing all nine men in Lieutenant Owen W. Winter Jr's crew. An explosion shortly before 8.30am on 6 January 1945 shook the town of Bury St. Edmunds. This was caused by bombs exploding from B-17G 42-97082 *Mission Mistress* in the 410th Bomb Squadron, which had crashed in a spinney between Mount Farm and Moreton Hall

On 30 November 1944 returning from a raid on Lutzkendorf, during landing peel-off at Rougham in rapidly deteriorating weather, two 94th Bomb Group Fortresses were on short final, one directly above the other and converging when the tower advised the aircraft on final to go around. 42-97985, the lower aircraft, piloted by Lieutenant Owen W. Winter, 331st Bomb Squadron, responded immediately and pulled up into the aircraft above. It crashed and burned in a nearby field and all except the tail gunner, who was critically injured, perished. The other aircraft crash-landed in a field without injury to the crew. *(Abe Dolim)*

Rougham airfield during an air show in the 1980s. *(Author)*

shortly after take-off from the main E–W runway after suffering engine failure. Five members of Lieutenant Jack W. Collins' crew were killed. The four others managed to scramble clear before the bombs exploded. Four crewmembers were killed on 28 January when B-17G 44-8600 in the 331st Squadron flown by Lieutenant Wilmar G. Weiss, crashed between the Thurston Road and the railway line.

Targets hit from January 1945 until the end of the war included Hamburg, Karlsruhe, Frankfurt Nuremberg, Bremen, Kiel and Berlin with the final mission to Ingolstadt on 21 April 1945. From May 1943 until April 1945, the 94th flew a total of 325 missions during which over 18,000 tons of bombs were delivered, 156 B-17s were lost in action and twenty-seven from other operational causes, though claims for enemy aircraft destroyed were also high. Of the 1,453 crewmembers shot down, 370 were killed and 162 wounded. The 94th Bomb Group left Rougham in December 1945. The station was transferred to the RAF on 20 December 1945 and finally returned to civil use in 1948. The control tower was occupied by a married couple from 1945 until the mid-to-late-1980s and then left empty for several more years.

Debach – Station 152

Construction of Debach airfield by the 820th and 829th Engineer Battalions (Aviation) of the US Army started on 11 September 1942 and was one of the last Eighth Air Force heavy bomber bases to be occupied. It was built to Air Ministry Directorate General Works (AMDGW) specification for a Class 'A' heavy bomber station and therefore followed the general pattern with a single 2,000-yard runway and two intersecting 1,400-yard runways. Two T2-type hangars and fifty hardstandings were erected for USAAF requirements. In common with other stations, built towards the latter end of the construction programme, the hardstandings were of the so-called 'spectacle' type rather than the 'frying-pan'. Accommodation was provided for 2,900 men in dispersed Nissen hut sites to the southwest of the field. Thistledon Hall, actually on the airfield itself, was taken over as an additional billet. The 493rd Bomb Group (named 'Helton's Hellcats' after the Group's first CO, Colonel Elbert Helton) began arriving on 10 May 1944 having flown from McCook airfield, Nebraska via Iceland and Ireland. Lieutenant John Shipley in the 860th squadron who, in his eagerness to be the first to land at Debach, overshot the runway and took out a petrol truck, which fortunately did not explode! John Lindquist, bombardier in Paul Berry's crew recalls:

Six crews landed that first day, before the airbase was actually finished. The control tower was not in operation and we picked our own runway, which turned out to be the longest but only 4,500 feet. We had trained on 9–10,000ft runways in the US and were a little surprised at such a short one.

Things did not improve much for Shipley's crew, as Rob Grandy, a gunner on the crew, explains:

On our second mission we crashed at Woodbridge landing strip and the plane was a total wreck. However, we did have an excuse this time as we were badly shot up.

The Group flew its first mission on D-Day. Altogether, thirty-six B-24s led by the CO, Colonel Helton, set out for Lisieux but 10/l0th cloud cover prevented the Group from bombing their target and all thirty-six B-24s returned with their bomb loads intact. Lieutenant Francis S. Milligan recalls: 'I guess we were too green to appreciate a "milk run"'. Then at 11,000ft, *No Love – No Nothing* in the 863rd Squadron, piloted by Captain Jack Cooper, struck the tail of *Moby Dick* in the 862nd Squadron, which was being flown by Lieutenant Donald L. Russell. *No Love – No Nothing* was seen to disintegrate and both Liberators disappeared into the overcast. Milligan adds, 'The sight sobered most of us'. There was only one survivor from Cooper's ship and none from Russell's. The death toll could have been higher; a piece of flak went through both the steel and cloth helmet worn by Sam Hale, the 861st Bomb Squadron commander, and

Little Warrior is shot down over Fallersleben, Germany on 29 June 1944. Staff Sergeant Clifford Stocking Jr in the 862nd Bomb Squadron, a waist gunner in *The Green Hornet*, took this dramatic photo. (*via Truett Woodall*)

lodged on top of his head. Two inches taller he would not have gone on to finish the twenty-six missions he flew. Lieutenant Joe Gualano, a pilot in the 860th Squadron, adds: 'It was said that "Lord Haw-Haw" that evening, announced that Germany had nothing to fear from the new Group with the "X" tail markings as they were killing themselves'.

The 93rd Combat Wing converted to the B-17G Fortress in late August 1944. The 12th September was the worst day in the brief history of the 493rd Bomb Group, which began the mission with thirty-eight B-17s. Lieutenant (later Captain) Roy L. Holtman in the 861st Bomb Squadron who flew deputy squadron lead to Captain Ellis Woodward was hoping to celebrate his 24th birthday.

What started out like any other mission, turned out to be the worst. The target, Magdeburg, a day to remember! We took off and assembled at altitude, as was standard procedure and departed on course for our target. We arrived at our IP and established our track to the target, experiencing very heavy flak. As we left the target, we were jumped by Focke Wulf 190s, supported by Me 109s, which we subsequently learned were one of Hitler's elite *Luftwaffe* Storm Groups.

Christmas party on the base. *(USAF)*

B-24 Liberators in the 493rd Bomb Group taxiing out. *(USAF)*

It seemed to take forever for the Low Squadron to make it through the intense flak since they were flying directly into a vicious headwind. Fortunately, all twelve aircraft emerged from the flak intact. But before the lead ship, Captain Woodward's aircraft, could close its bomb bay doors that had been damaged by flak, a force of twenty or more Fw 190s escorted by an equal number of Bf 109s, seemed to appear out of the flak and attacked the squadron from the rear. In moments seven B-17s were either spiralling down or descending on fire. The five remaining B-17s received varying degrees of damage but remained under control. The Fortress gunners from the five remaining aircraft made a valiant effort and claimed as many as four German fighters as they fended off their attackers. Continued German attacks succeeded in dispersing these remaining Fortresses and each sustained major damage.

Staff Sergeant Hayward F. Deese Jnr., engineer–left waist gunner in Lieutenant George M. Durgin's crew in *Ulpy* in the 863rd Bomb Squadron recalls:

After the bomb run Fw 190s with 20mm cannons hit us from the rear. On their first pass they shot down nine out of the twelve B-17s in the Squadron. Our B-17 and two wing crews were left. The fighters came after us, shot down the wing crews and shot us up with 20mm cannon and 13mm machine gun fire. I got three pieces of 20mm in my back and Don Gray, right waist-gunner, had a 20mm bullet explode in his face and 13mm slugs in each leg. (I was standing on two flak vests and when I picked them up to return them after the mission there was a hole about 8-inches diameter under them and a lot of 20mm shrapnel right where I had been standing. The flak vests were in shreds. They saved my legs and my life). Durgin called me to look at the left elevator for damage. I knew what was wrong because I put a burst of 50 calibre through it shooting at an Me 109.

The Low 'C' Squadron was led by lead crew pilot Captain Ellis M. Woodward and his co-pilot 1st Lieutenant William C. Rawson in *Ramp Happy Pappy*, which took 'a jillion hits but kept on flying'. Woodward recalled:

We dropped our bombs, cleared the flak area over the target, breathed a sigh of relief, turned left and headed for home. But our relief was to be short-lived. Over the intercom came the dreaded word, 'fighters'. We were leading a flight of twelve B-17s. Within 60 seconds, we could feel some of the hits from 20mm cannon shells ripping through the airplane. And within 90 seconds of the warning we looked around and found that there was no one left in our squadron except us and our deputy lead, our right wingman and us. All the other ten B-17s had disappeared, each with nine crewmen aboard. What a catastrophe! Arithmetically, that amounted to a loss of one human being per second.

The arrival of P-51s finally forced the Germans to break off their engagements with the bombers. The dispersed, crippled Forts

B-24J *Flamin Mamie* was flown by Lieutenant Ambrose C. Shaw in the 862nd Bomb Squadron, while on Temporary Duty (TDY) flying gas haul to the continent with the 27th Air Transport Group at Lyneham near Salisbury, Wiltshire in 1944. *(USAF)*

B-24J-155-CO 44-40286 *The Green Hornet*, which later served in the 491st Bomb Group. *(USAF)*

B-24J-155-CO 44-40298 *The Shack* in the 861st Bomb Squadron, 493rd Bomb Group is a clever pun on the name of Ann Shackleford who was the fiancée of Captain David L. 'Doc' Conger, the pilot. This Liberator was one of several that were transferred to the 2nd Bomb Division in the summer of 1944 when the 3rd Bomb Division converted fully to the B-17 and *The Shack* joined the 458th Bomb Group. *(USAF)*

B-24H 42-94857 *Big Dealer* in the
493rd Bomb Group in 1944.
(USAF)

B-24J-155-CO 44-40299 in the 860th Bomb Squadron, 493rd Bomb Group
was named *Purty Baby* by the crew and painted by Sergeant Duane
Bryers. It flew to England in April 1944. On 25 June, with two engines out,
Lieutenant Daigle crash-landed the aircraft at the emergency airfield
at Woodbridge after returning from St Avord, France. The aircraft
was salvaged and repaired and transferred to the 487th Bomb Group
before being assigned to the MTO on 3 December 1944 by BAD2.
(via Truett Woodall)

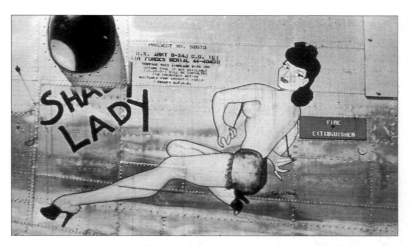

B-24J-160-CO 44-40439 *Shady Lady* served in the 493rd and 34th Bomb
Groups until they converted to the Fortress and it was reallocated to
the 567th Bomb Squadron, 389th Bomb Group. *Shady Lady* and
2nd Lieutenant George S. Crock's crew FTR from the mission to
Brunswick on 31 March 1945 when they were shot down by a pair of
Me 262s. All nine crew were KIA. *(USAF)*

then set course for Allied occupied territory while tending to
wounded crewmen and assessing their damage. Two of the five
landed at Brussels to get aid for critically wounded crewmen and
to land their damaged aircraft. The other three elected to return
the wounded to England since their aircraft seemed airworthy
for the flight across the Channel. On reaching England Captain
Woodward elected to land at the emergency landing strip at
Woodbridge because of damage that affected the flight controls of
Ramp Happy Pappy. As soon as the crew made their exit *Ramp
Happy Pappy* was towed off the landing strip and dumped in the
junk heap. Only two aircraft in the low squadron made it back to
Debach.

The legacy of Magdeburg extended to the German defences
guarding other cities in their homeland and during 13 September–
25 November 1944 they were responsible for the loss of eleven
493rd Bomb Group crews over Germany.

The worst accident to occur at Debach took place on 12 December
1944 when *Devils Own* piloted by Lieutenant John F. DeWitt

B-24J-160-CO 44-40437 *Hairless Joe* in the 860th Bomb Squadron, 493rd
Bomb Group with three P-51B Mustangs in the 363rd Fighter Squadron,
357th Fighter Group. *Hairless Joe* was named after the maker of 'Kickapoo
Joy Juice' in Al Capp's legendary satirical comic strip *Li'l Abner*, which
had started in the Depression year of 1934. The Liberator was transferred
to the 44th Bomb Group when the 3rd Bomb Division converted to
Fortresses and it FTRLOC (Failed to Return – Landed on the Continent)
on 30 November 1944. *(USAF)*

B-17G-65-VE 44-8452 in the 493rd Bomb Group over Haarlem
during 'Chowhound' food drops to the starving Dutch population on
2 May 1945 when forty B-17s led by Lieutenant Colonel Shepler
W. Fitzgerald, deputy Group commander, dropped 3,510 cases of food.
(USAF via Truett Woodall)

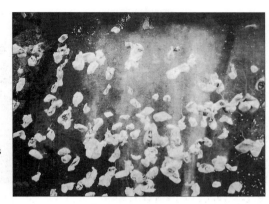

Sacks of flour being dropped over Haarlem, Holland on 3 May 1945. Two days later the Germans in Holland surrendered. *(via Truett Woodall)*

was gaining height after taking off for a mission to Darmstadt. One engine burst into flames and, unable to maintain height and with the threat of the imminent collapse of the port wing, DeWitt had no option but to bring the B-17 straight in. He narrowly missed a parked Fortress and an army truck before belly landing alongside the runway. As the aircraft came to a halt, the burning wing folded back setting fire to the fuselage. The crew managed to escape to safety before the entire bomb load exploded two minutes later. The blast was bad enough to damage several buildings and lift the doors from off the nearby T2 hangar.

493rd Bomb Group veterans return to Debach before the restoration of the control tower. *(Author)*

The former movie theatre at Debach airfield near Clopton, Suffolk by Grove Farm, where 'Helton's Hellcats' of the 493rd Bomb Group were based during 1944–1945. *(Author)*

Unfortunately the American engineers had not made a very satisfactory job of constructing the runway and the concrete soon started to break up. By the end of the year, the position was so bad that the group had to move temporarily to Little Walden while runways were repaired and strengthened. The group returned to Debach in March 1945 and it flew its last combat operation on 20 April.

The old control tower at Debach has now been restored and is a museum. *(Author)*

Memorabilia in the Debach Tower Museum. *(Author)*

Memorabilia in the Debach Tower Museum. *(Author)*

After the US forces returned home, Debach was used first as a camp for German PoWs and later for displaced persons before being abandoned about 1948. It was sold in 1963–64, the main N–S runway becoming the boundary between two adjoining

Debach airfield in June 2006. *(Author)*

farms. Both of the T2 hangers were removed before the sale. In 1969 the Northern end of the main runway was sold to build a mushroom farm, this being disbanded in the mid-seventies. The mushroom farm was later sold and used for grain and general storage. Much of the concrete runways and taxiways were taken up and crushed for use in road building and the land reclaimed for agriculture. Many of the buildings on the technical site fell down and some were later restored. Others were built on the old sites and on the site of the T2 hangar, which is now a farm grain store. The control tower, which was vandalized over many years was restored and is now a museum. The historic Thistledon Hall, which was also vandalized during its wartime occupation, with most of the interior panelling and staircases being burnt for firewood, was only fit for demolition after the war. Only the foundations now remain in the undergrowth of the copse on the southern corner of the airfield. The firm St. Ives Sand & Gravel removed some concrete. Pylons carrying electricity from the atomic power station at Sizewell now cross the southern edge of the former airfield.

3

Deopham Green –
Station 142

To the east of the forested and heathland area of Norfolk known as the Breckland, lies Deopham Green. After requisition Mr. Jeffrey of Stalland Farm was left with only 45 acres from his original 100-acre farm. The airfield was constructed during 1942–1943 by John Laing & Sons Ltd to Class 'A' specification, with a 2,000-yard main runway and two intersecting 1,400-yard auxiliary runways. Fifty hardstandings were provided; two T2-type hangars, one at each side of the airfield; Mark II airfield lighting on the main runway and full technical facilities and accommodation in

B-17G-45-BO 42-97083 *Flatbush Floogie* in the 728th Bomb Squadron, crash-landed at Jadebusen, Germany on the shore of the Baltic on the mission to Rostock on 11 April 1944. Lieutenant Thomas L. Gardner's crew were taken prisoner. *(via Hans-Heiri Stapfer)*

B-17G-35-DL 42-107091 *Forbidden Fruit* of 728th Bomb Squadron, which suffered flak damage on the mission on 8 May 1944. On 17 February 1945 *Forbidden Fruit* crashed after a mid-air collision while forming up. Joe Knoll and five of his crew were killed. *(TAMM)*

temporary buildings for 2,900 men. Some 500,000 cubic yards of soil were excavated during construction and 223,000 cubic yards of concrete laid down, plus 32,000 square yards of tarmac surfacing. Six miles of hedges and 1,400 trees were removed from the site. The 452nd Bomb Group occupied the airfield on 3 January 1944 and the group started flying B-17 combat missions from the base on 5 February. The group flew a total of 250 missions from Deopham Green during the war, losing 110 of its bombers in combat.

On 12 May 1944 on the mission to Brux the Americans reported the loss of forty-six bombers. Worst hit was the 45th Combat Bombardment Wing, the 452nd lost fourteen Fortresses. *Lucky Lady*, piloted by 1st Lieutenant Dick Noble, was one of these, as Staff Sergeant Ralph J. Munn the ball turret gunner recalls:

There was the usual amount of flak but no fighters until we were quite deep into Germany. As usual, the enemy was reluctant to attack until our P 47s and P 38 escorts made the turn for home base. Until just short of target we had considerable action, mostly high-level attacks down through the squadron. When we reached the IP the flak was a solid carpet. Up to this point we had not had any damage outside of small to fist-size holes. I had always made it a practice to turn my turret to 12 o' clock when the bomb-bay doors opened. Bruce dropped a salvo and at the same time Dick turned into the down-wind leg. We were hardly off the target when we took a direct hit in the bomb bay area. In the meantime I had turned around to 6 o'clock to see what was happening. A fraction of a second later, there was another very bad jolt. This one knocked out my source of power, my electrical suit boots and gloves. I was hit in the back and the turret took considerable damage. My guns and intercom were out. It was slippery in the turret. I was then aware that I was isolated and had no control over what was to happen next. The second hit took out the left inboard engine and the ball turret. The engine out was an invitation for the remaining fighters to attack. I think that with the bomb bay doors down, they assumed we were damaged badly enough that they could work on a more active victim. I did not see another fighter until we reached the mountain foothills in eastern Belgium. Within a matter of minutes we all evacuated the *Not So Lucky Lady*. Surprisingly it was a very orderly departure, no hesitations either; all of us had had enough for that day.

The 452nd Bomb Group suffered particularly heavy losses during the spring of 1944, at that time sustaining one of the highest rates of loss of any Fortress group in the Eighth Air Force. On 21 April B-17G *Little Chum* in the 729th Bomb Squadron crashed at Hoxne in Suffolk, with six crew killed, after entering a thundercloud. On 19 May B-17G 42-38145 in the 730th Squadron was involved in a collision over Old Buckenham with a 388th Bomb Group B-17 killing two of Lieutenant William C. Gaither's crew. On 21 June 1944 the 452nd were part of the shuttle to Russia and their target en route was an oil refinery at Ruhland, Germany. At Poltava German bombing that evening was a massacre and fourty-four of the seventy-two Fortresses that had landed there were destroyed on the ground. On 26 October two of the Group's B-17Gs were involved in a collision at Caston Hall, Norfolk with sixteen men killed and both tail gunners injured. There was another accident on 17 February 1945 when *Forbidden Fruit* hit

Bombs fall from the bomb bays of B-17G-35-DL 42-107091 *Forbidden Fruit* in the 728th Bomb Squadron, over Schwerte, Germany on 31 May 1944. Earlier that month Captain Edward Starka had put the B-17 down at Rattlesden on 8 May after flak had killed his rear gunner. *Forbidden Fruit* crash-landed on 17 February 1945 and was salvaged on 21 May 1945.
(via Sam Young)

propwash just after take-off and did a barrell-roll before crashing near Tibenham. Only three men baled out after being thrown clear. The last wartime loss was on 20 April 1945 when *Slienthe Je Vahr*, a 731st Bomb Squadron Fortress flown by 1st Lieutenant George V. Pringle, a veteran of twenty-nine missions, was involved in a mid-air collision with Lieutenant Delmar Hallet's B-17.

The loss of B-17G 42-97904 *Lady Jeanette* in the 729th Bomb Squadron on 9 November 1944 during an attack on the marshalling yards at Saarbrücken, resulted in Medal of Honor awards to the 21-year old pilot, 1st Lieutenant Donald J. Gott and his co-pilot, 2nd Lieutenant William F. Metzger. The Fortress had three engines badly damaged and the number one engine set on fire. It began windmilling and the No. 2 engine was failing rapidly. Number four showered flames back towards the tail assembly. Flares were ignited in the cockpit and the flames were fuelled by hydraulic fluid leaking from severed cables. Technical Sergeant Russell W. Gustafson, the engineer/top-turret gunner was wounded in the leg and a shell fragment had severed

1st Lieutenant Donald J. Gott and 2nd Lieutenant William F. Metzger, 729th Bomb Squadron, whose actions on 9 November 1944 resulted in posthumous awards of the Medal of Honor.

Technical Sergeant Robert A. Dunlap, the radio operator's arm below his elbow. Metzger left his seat and stumbled back to the radio room and applied a tourniquet to stop the bleeding. However, Dunlap was so weak from pain that he fell unconscious. The bombs were still aboard and Gott was faced with the prospect of the aircraft exploding at any moment. He therefore decided to fly the stricken Fortress to Allied territory a few miles distant

B-17G-35-BO 42-32083 *Flatbush Floogie* which on 26 February 1945 was shot down by fighters and flak and crashed at Zossen. All nine of 2nd Lieutenant Allan A. Marksian's crew survived and they returned. *(TAMM)*

Robin Hood kneeling on a lintel (left) and Robin Hood's Merrie men
(right) in the former library. *(Author)*

and attempt a crash landing. The bombs were salvoed over
enemy territory and all excess equipment was thrown overboard.
Metzger unselfishly gave his parachute to 2nd Lieutenant John
A. Harland, navigator, after his had been damaged in the fire. As
Lady Jeanette neared friendly territory, Metzger went to the rear

Robin Hood and Little John in what was the American base library at
Deopham Green airfield and which is now a carpentry shop.

The stage is set but sadly, these 6ft high dancing girls at Deopham Green disappeared in the late seventies when the building was demolished.
(Author)

'Bandy legged cowboy' recalls a time when American airmen at Deopham Green had great artists in their midst. *(Author)*

This Micky Mouse cartoon once glamorised the far wall of a Nissen hut at Deopham Green together with other Disney creations. *(Author)*

of the Fortress and told everyone to bale out. Staff Sergeant Herman B. Krimminger, tail gunner, died when his parachute opened accidentally and snagged the blazing B-17's tailplane when he was pulled outside the bomber. Metzger then went back to his seat and the two pilots prepared for a crash landing with only one engine still functioning and the other three on fire. An open field was spotted and Gott brought *Lady Jeanette* in at Hattonville 20 miles south-west of Verdun. At about 100ft the fire took hold of the fuel tanks and the bomber exploded, killing Gott, Metzger, and Technical Sergeant Robert A. Dunlap instantly. Both pilots were awarded posthumous Medals of Honor.

2nd Lieutenant Joseph F. Harms, bombardier, John A. Harland, Staff Sergeants James O. Fross, ball-turret gunner, and William R. Robbins, right waist-gunner and Technical Sergeant Russell Gustafson, the last man to bale out, all survived. Gustafson landed about half a mile from the crash scene. He recalled:

> Fortunately the air was heavy and my descent was slow and I was able to land without further injury. After a few minutes on the ground, two Frenchmen came up to me and offered to give aid. Another four or five minutes brought an American ambulance and I was on my way to a field hospital. The next 12–13 months were spent in army hospitals putting my leg back together. After receiving a medical discharge I closed the door on the war.

The 452nd returned to the USA during July and August 1945 and the station was handed back to RAF Maintenance Command on 9 October 1945. Public roads, closed when construction started in 1942, were later reopened, one of them using part of the old main runway, the airfield finally being abandoned on 1 January 1948. Negotiations for the repurchase of the former airfield began in 1961–62 and gradually the land was returned to agriculture though the control tower, administration buildings and the hangars have long since disappeared.

4

Eye (Brome) – Station 134

For several centuries the site of this airfield was part of the Cornwallis estate. The surrender by the Marquis of Cornwallis at Yorktown in 1781 had meant victory for the Americans in the War of Independence. Eye was one of the last Class 'A' airfields to be built for the US Eighth Air Force. Construction began in 1943 jointly by the American 827th and 829th Engineer Battalions and British contractors and was completed in early 1944. Three intersecting runways, perimeter track and thirty dispersed hardstandings were laid down, with the technical, administration and living accommodation buildings built mainly to the north-east of the airfield and extending to the village of Brome. Part of the perimeter track ran parallel with the main Norwich–Ipswich A140 road with eight of the hardstandings sited on the side opposite the main runway. It became a regular occurrence for road traffic to be halted by military police to allow a B-24 or B-17 to trundle across the road to these dispersal points.

The 490th Bombardment Group, which was commanded by Colonel Lloyd H. Watnee and equipped with B-24H and B-24J Liberators, arrived on 26 April 1944 to become part of the 93rd Combat Wing, joining the 34th Bomb Group at Mendlesham and the 493rd Bomb Group at Debach. The 490th Bomb Group's early missions were of a tactical nature in support of the Normandy landings, but their first mission on 31 May when 1,029 heavies were dispatched, had to be abandoned after the Group encountered thick cloud and became so dispersed after emerging from the cloud that the Group was recalled. One Liberator dropped its bomb load on a German airfield near Rotterdam. Thereafter, targets were mainly in the strategic role to industrial, oil and communications sites in Germany and occupied Europe, which included Cologne, Hamburg, Münster, Kassel and Berlin. In June Colonel Frank P. Bostrom took command of the Group and he remained at the helm until June 1945. On 7 June when German intruders were over East Anglia, two B-24s in the 490th Bomb Group were wrecked in a runway collision at RAF Feltwell. By early August 1944 the 490th Bomb Group had flown forty missions. In August–September the 490th Bomb Group began conversion from the Liberator to the B-17G Fortress, as did the other B-24H/J Liberator-equipped groups in the 92nd and 93rd Combat Wings. The changeover period was brief and the 490th Bomb Group returned to combat action by the end of August. The 'T in a square' on the rudders of the B-24s was replaced by plus signs and a 'U', with red-tipped fins and a red band on each wing and tailplane.

B-17G 44-6893 *Looky Looky* in the 851st Bomb Squadron in 1945. *(USAF)*

Lieutenant Wallace Johnson in the 490th recalls the mission of Tuesday 17 October:

I was flying our B-17 *Big Poison* on a mission to the marshalling yards at Cologne when we took an almost direct flak hit that severed all the oil lines on No. 2 engine, including the one to the feathering pump. Consequently all attempts to feather that engine were futile; this caused extreme over-speeding of the prop and with no oil to the engine it soon seized, causing the crankshaft to shear. This left me with one prop running wild (windmilling), causing a huge amount of drag which I could not overcome, even with the other three engines at full power. As we dropped out of formation we were picked up and escorted by two little friends, P-51s. As pilot-in-command it was up to me at this point to make the decision to try and make the Channel crossing back home to Eye or attempt a landing on the Continent. I reasoned that there was a high risk of the runaway prop breaking away from its mount and slicing through the nose of the aircraft, with dire consequences. I also knew that there was a possibility I would have to ditch the plane in the Channel. Either way, concern for the safety of my crew made me decide to land at Brussels. Maintenance crews came out to meet us and their inspection revealed that the prop was ready to fall off with the touch of a finger. I was glad that I had made the right decision.

On 22nd October Lieutenant Kenneth H. French, bombardier in Lieutenant Curtis R. McKinney's crew in the 490th Bomb Group flew his 22nd mission.

Today we had a fairly easy mission to Münster. We briefed at 0700 hours and took off at 1011 hours in a ground fog with 1,000-yard visibility. We climbed to 18,000ft where we joined in formation with our squadron and then took a course across the North Sea. Our fighter support was good; they left us when we were past the fighter danger zone and continued on with the boys who were going to Hanover and Brunswick. There were no enemy fighters seen or reported. After a flak-free run over Holland we reached the target area at about 1445 hours and as we flew past Osnabrück the flak really

started. They were sending up a good box barrage and plenty
of rockets but thank God we didn't get mixed up in it. We
had a box barrage directly in front of us on the target (we had
been briefed for seventy guns) but we turned off to the left
to make the run. They sent up more flak but it was low and to
the rear of us and we suffered no damage. About twelve
rockets came up, right at our altitude and fairly accurate. I
saw one explode at Osnabrück and it looked like a flash of
lightning.

On Thursday 30 November when about 1,200 heavies set out to
bomb four synthetic-oil refineries in Germany the 3rd Division
were given Merseburg and flak shot down thirteen bombers.
The losses affected men and morale. Lieutenant Jule F. Berndt,
navigator in Lieutenant Rolland B. Peacock Jnr's crew in the 850th
Bomb Squadron had remained on base with the co-pilot of the
crew of *Magnificent Obsession* even though they had been given a
pass. The young navigator was deeply affected.

When we learned during the afternoon that our boys had
gone to Merseburg we went to the flight line to await their
return. 'Sweating out' the return of the planes is quite some
experience. Many of the crews and other personnel began
to gather around the time that the formation was expected to
return. At about 1630 hours we saw the first ships approaching from the east. They were the Chaff ships that precede
the other formations over the target. As they landed we could
see that all these planes were in good condition and we
anxiously awaited the other bombers. It was with some
anxiety that we counted the number of ships in the formation
when it came into sight. Of the thirty-six that we knew had
been dispatched we could count only twenty-four and we
wondered whether fighters had struck our group. When
all the aircraft had landed we went to the hardstand where
ours was parked to see what damage *Magnificent Obsession*
had sustained. First of all we questioned the crew on the
opposition they had encountered. The navigator told us that
they had flown through 13 minutes of flak that was the
most concentrated of any mission. Fortunately our plane had
received only two hits. The 490th had led the 8th Air Force

over the target with our CO, Colonel Bostrom, riding in the lead ship. Just before the target, the lead ship's pathfinding equipment became inoperative and another plane had to take over. Because of this, or perhaps due to faulty navigation, the formation missed the IP and ran into the flak areas beyond. Immediately a flak barrage was put up that many of the old crews termed as the heaviest they had ever witnessed. All the way into the target and for a time after bombs away, the planes were under constant fire of concentrated, accurate flak. Of the thirty-six planes that the 490th sent over, thirty-one of them received major battle damage but thankfully not a single one went down.

On the second Schweinfurt raid on 14 October 1943 the 3rd Division dropped the most bombs on target and the 390th Bomb Group was the most successful. Despite the lead ship experiencing difficulty, all fifteen aircraft placed 50 per cent of their bombs within 1,000ft of the MPI. The 3rd Division lost fifteen aircraft. Gus Mencow, lead navigator, 520th Bomb Squadron, recalled later:

We got fifteen planes over Schweinfurt. One was lost to a combination of flak and fighters. Other groups did not fare so well. The flak was extremely thick but fortunately the *Luftwaffe* concentrated on other groups. When we got back to base and learned of the high losses it turned out to be a sad day. The week was just too much for all of us and Schweinfurt put the finishing touch. We felt convinced that getting through the war was impossible but somehow we carried on.

On 11 December the weather cleared sufficiently for the heavies to set out for Emden. Rocket-firing Bf 110s and Me 210s made persistent attacks on the bomber formations and seventeen heavies were shot down, including *Six Nights in Telergma*, the lead ship piloted by Captain Hiram Skogmo in the 390th Bomb Group. Captain Irving Lifson, one of the two navigators on board, recalls:

We were feigning a raid on the Heligoland area, hoping to draw the enemy fighter planes up towards Denmark. Then we were to cut back on Emden. Shortly after turning back onto Emden eight Me 110s came through the formation, firing rockets. We were hit right away and set on fire. There were eleven of us on board and only Captain Donald Warren and myself the Group Navigator (who landed on the island of Nordeney) survived. German marines picked us up. Ernest Phillips, a gunner, landed in the North Sea and was picked up by a boat. Among those lost was Major Ralph V. Hansell, the 390th Operations Officer, the strike leader who was flying as co-pilot. I spent the rest of the war in *Stalag Luft I* Barth.

On 25 February 1944 during 'Big Week' the USSTAF and the 3rd Division returned to Regensburg for the first time since 17 August 1943 when the B-17s had suffered such devastating losses, *Oberfeldwebel* 'Addi' Glunz of JG26 claimed *Liberty Belle-E* in the 570th Bomb Squadron flown by Lieutenant George Rains. 2nd Lieutenant Robert V. McCalmont, a bombardier in the 390th, witnessed the gallant Fortress pilot trying desperately to save his bomber.

I watched this guy do everything but a snap roll to shake off four Germans who were out with everything they had to get him. He dived, climbed and banked and one time went so close to the ground that plane and shadow seemed to converge [sic]. He headed back up again with one fighter still hugging his tail and levelled off below us. His last message came through our earphones: 'That's all brother, you're looking at my last engine!' The ship's nose pitched forward and a minute later it crashed and burned.

On 29 February when 215 B-17s bombed production plants at Brunswick again *Oberfeldwebel* Wilhelm Mayer of JG 26 attacked *Ole Basser*, a B-17 in the 570th Bomb Squadron, and shot it down while taking hits in the cockpit. Five of 2nd Lieutenant Everett J. Ferguson's crew were killed. The other five baled out and one evaded but the others were captured.

In 1944 the 390th Bomb Group took part in many rough missions, including the March Berlin series of missions and raids on oil targets, including 12 May when the five main oil plants were attacked and the Group was among those, that carried out the long and gruelling mission to the oil refinery complex at Brüx. On 7 June during the German intruder attack on East Anglia, the Group was returning from the mission to Tours and Nantes late in the evening. It was about dusk and the B-24s were just south of the base when over the radio came the call, "All Clambake yellow aircraft do not land. Red bandits! Red bandits! Red bandits!" None of the 490th aircraft were lost but *Madame Shoo Shoo* and *Flying Ginnie* did have serious accidents while landing at the nearly blacked out diversionary aircraft at Feltwell near Thetford.

During July the 8th flew missions to Germany in search of oil and other strategic targets in an ever-diminishing Reich. On 7 July Nick G. Plackis flew his first deep penetration after making a few short haul sorties that proved to be milk runs, giving the crew the false impression that combat flying was a 'piece of cake'. But that was to change quickly on 7 July when they were exposed to their first 'blood-bath' before ever getting near the target at Merseburg. Plackis says:

> We had just crossed the English Channel and still over the Zuider Zee above Holland when our two wingmen on the right collided due to propwash turbulence while tightening up our formation, one directly on top of the other. It was like a slow motion movie. When the upper B-17 descended into the wings of the lower one, its props chewed into the aluminum while the lower B-17's props were disintegrating the belly of the upper one. Gasoline was spewing everywhere and immediately ignited both aircraft into bright orange flaming torches. The No. 2 prop of the upper plane broke off cleanly at the shaft in one piece and as it came off, it laid flat on the top of the wing as it slowly slid off into space. We watched in horror, as both flaming B-17s gently peeled off to the right, together, prior to going into a joined spin. We counted five chutes before both planes separated. The lower one exploded in a tremendous blast with a full load of bombs, maximum long haul fuel and ten crew. The other Fortress blew up a short distance from the first, but we heard that some of the crew who baled out were captured and became PoWs.

In December 1944 the 490th Bomb Group took part in the 'Battle of the Bulge' and also made a number of supply and leaflet

B-24H-20-FO 42-94953 *Rugged But Right* (later *Misanthrope*), which served in the 490th Bomb Group and the 715th Bomb Squadron, 448th Bomb Group before being scrapped at Altus, Oklahoma in late 1945. *(USAF)*

drops. On 17 March 1945 when 1,328 B-17s and B-24s, escorted by 820 fighters, bombed targets in west and north-central Germany, the 490th Bomb Group was returning from a raid on Bittefeld when they encountered cirrus clouds which forced them to fly on instruments for 30 minutes. The Fortresses moved into tighter formation. Suddenly, a squadron in the 385th Bomb Group cut through the clouds into the 490th formation, causing one of the 490th ships, flown by Lieutenant Arthur Stern, to veer upwards. In no time at all it collided with another 490th B-17, flown by Lieutenant Robert H. Tennenberg. The radio room in the lower Fortress took the full force of the collision and the aircraft broke in two. All nine of Stern's crew were killed. In Tennenberg's Fortress, 'Chester A. Deptula', the navigator, dragged the stunned nose-gunner, John Gann, from the shattered nose to the radio operator's compartment. Despite a smashed engine, another partly disabled, a wing-tip bent, the front of the nose knocked off and the pilot's front view window broken, Tennenberg kept his B-17 airborne and managed to reach Belgium where he made a successful crash-landing. The crewmen stepped out unhurt and surveyed the damage. Amongst the wreckage was the mutilated torso of a man later identified as the radio operator from the Fortress that had collided with them. He had been forced through the shattered Plexiglas nose of Tennenberg's aircraft on impact.

In one of the last air battles of the European war the Group lost four aircraft to two Me 262 jets while over Prague and en route to hit marshalling yards at Aussig. The two Me 262 were in turn shot down by P-51 Mustangs. By the war's end the 490th Bomb Group had flown 138 combat missions and had dropped a total of over 12,000 tons of bombs and 9 tons of leaflets, in addition to the supplies dropped to Partisans and food to the starving Dutch during operation 'Chowhound'.

The 490th Bomb Group had the distinction of holding the record for the lowest number of aircraft missing in action (twenty-two) while a further thirty-two aircraft were lost to other operational causes. During a practice mission on the afternoon of Friday 5 January 1945 when approaching the north-eastern outskirts of Bury St. Edmunds, two B-17Gs in the 849th Bomb Squadron, 43-38111 flown by 2nd Lieutenant Donald L. Wood and 45-38050, piloted by 2nd Lieutenant Harold Adelman, collided. Wood's aircraft spun in and crashed in the Merrimaid Pits (small lakes for purifying effluent pumped from the Bury Sugar Beet Factory) on the eastern boundary of the town. All nine crew were killed and it took several days to recover the bodies from the icy water.

P-51D Mustang *Big Beautiful Doll* passing Eye (Brome) airfield. *(Author)*

Eye (Brome) airfield in 2008. *(Author)*

Adelman's Fortress broke up into hundreds of pieces. He and six of his crew, including one crewmember who baled out with his parachute on fire and fell to his death, were killed.

The 490th Bomb Group returned to the USA in July–August 1945 and Eye was returned to RAF Bomber Command on 1 November 1945. The airfield was gradually run down ever the next five years and was eventually sold off in 1962–63. A number of light industrial concerns have occupied some of the buildings since that time including firms engaged in straw-board manufacture and mushroom farming among others. Parts of the concrete surfaces were broken up for hardcore for local roads, although up until late 1986 the runway was usable by microlights and light aircraft. In more recent times Eye was used for Sunday markets until a natural gas pumping station was established on the airfield.

5

Fersfield (Winfarthing) – Station 554 (Formerly 140)

This airfield was not an independent USAAF base but a satellite for Knettishall, the base for the 388th Bombardment Group. Fersfield airfield comprised a 2,000-yard long SW–NE runway and two auxiliary runways 1,400 yards long running N–S and SE–NW respectively, a perimeter track, and two hangars and fifty hardstandings. The base area lay to the southwest.

It was at Fersfield that the USAAF Project Aphrodite and US Navy administered Project Anvil pilotless drone operations using war-weary B-17s and PB4Y-1 Liberators respectively were launched. Each aircraft was packed with 18,000lb of Torpex, a nitroglycerine compound, and was flown to a point over the English coast or North Sea. There the pilot and co-pilot baled out, leaving the drone to fly on and be directed onto its target (normally a V1 or V2 site) by remote control via a Ventura 'mother ship'. Strike analysis depended upon the films brought back by accompanying Mosquitoes of the 25th Bomb group at Watton, Norfolk to determine the success, or failure, of the mission. Each Aphrodite and Anvil mission was preceded by a Bluestocking weather reconnaissance flight over the target by a 653rd Bomb Squadron Mosquito. After the drone was airborne, a Mosquito joined the mission carrying an 8th Combat Camera Unit (CCU)

BBMF Spitfire XIX PS915 photographed from the rear turret of Lancaster BI PA474 with Fersfield airfield in the background on Battle of Britain Day, 15 September 1999. *(Author)*

crewman. The mission was to fly close to the drone and to photograph its flight and its effects.

The first four drones were launched from Fersfield on 4 August 1944. One of these got no further than Sudbourne Park, Suffolk, where it crashed into a wood causing a terrific explosion and creating a crater of 100ft diameter. The remainder reached their target areas but only moderate results were achieved, as was the case two days later when two more drones were dispatched to Watten in France.

The two projects were not successful. A number of the aircraft crashed and many pilots were killed, including Lieutenant Joe Kennedy USN, elder brother of John F. Kennedy, on 12 August when his PB4Y-1 Liberator was headed for Heligoland. On reaching the Blyth estuary, just prior to Kennedy and his co-pilot Bud Willy baling out, the Liberator exploded at 13,000ft. Nothing except a few metal fragments was ever recovered from this disaster which caused blast detonation to property over an area of about 6 miles.

Another experimental project at Fersfield was Operation Batty, which consisted of two TV guided flying-bombs fitted onto the undercarriage of a B-17. The 388th Bomb Group operated B-17 Flying Fortresses and was given the task of administering the 'Batty' projects, which were mounted from Fersfield from 12 July until the end of 1944, providing base and maintenance facilities. The 563rd Bomb Squadron handled the administration and provision of personnel for this project. Three attempts were made in 1944 to use these against U-boat pens but they too were not successful, and the project was abandoned. The USAAF left Fersfield in late 1944. The RAF returned briefly on 21 March 1945 to operate three FB.VI Mosquito squadrons of 140 Wing (21 RAF, 464 RAAF and 487 RNZAF Squadrons), 2nd Tactical Air Force against the Shellhaus Gestapo building in Copenhagen. Fersfield airfield was closed in December 1945 and subsequently sold.

6

Framlingham (Parham) – Station 153

F ramlingham (also known as Parham) was built during 1942–1943 as a standard heavy bomber airfield to Class 'A' specification. The three intersecting runways were of 2,030, 1,440 and 1,430 yards length and there was a concrete perimeter track and fifty hardstandings, plus two T2 hangars, technical sites and Nissen hut accommodation for 3,000 personnel dispersed in the surrounding countryside. No part of the airfield fell within the boundary of Framlingham parish, the site being three miles to the east between the villages of Great Glemham and Parham, with all the technical sites, administrative buildings and living sites around Silverlace Green. The base was first occupied by the 95th Bomb Group, which was commanded by Colonel Alfred A. Kessler, on 12 May 1943. The facilities were still incomplete and the air echelon did not move to Framlingham until the end of May, having flown missions from Alconbury. The 95th flew its first mission on 13 May 1943. Two day's later the 95th Bomb Group's last mission from Essex was a disaster. Almost all the enemy fighters concentrated on the 4th Wing's seventy-six B-17s heading for Kiel in four combat boxes. On the approach to the target the fight started. Riding in the co-pilot's seat of the command aircraft flown by Captain Harry A Stirwalt in the 95th Bomb Group at the head of the Wing was Brigadier General Nathan

Cartoons from Army Talk 1944.

Bedford Forrest III from 402nd Combat Bomb Wing (P) Head-quarters. Forrest was the grandson of a very famous Confederate cavalry general in the American Civil War, whose motto had been, 'To win, git there fustest with the mostest'. On Forrest's instigation the seventeen B-17s of the 95th Bomb Group's main formation (seven more flew in the Composite Group formation) were flying a hitherto untried 'flat' formation, wing-tip to wing-tip, supposedly to be able to concentrate firepower ahead, below, above and to the rear more effectively. Bf 109Gs and FW190s attacked the Fortresses just after the bomb run. Many of the Fortress gunners were unable to return fire as their guns, which were lubricated with a new type of oil recommended by Forrest, had frozen. A massive diving frontal attack raked the lead aircraft with cannon fire from one end to the other and Stirwalt's ship fell out of formation and spiralled down. Four of the six B-17s in the low squadron were shot down. Two more were lost from the High Squadron and three more from the Composite Group formation brought the group's losses to ten (an eleventh crashed in England). Captain John Miller, 412th Bomb Squadron Operations Officer in the 95th Bomb Group and pilot of the severely damaged Fortress, *T'Ain't A Bird*, recalls that the news that 102 flight crewmembers were MIA had a stunning impact on his group commander. Following a thoroughly depressing and sad briefing during which he listened to the accounts of the surviving crews in silence, Colonel Kessler, his eyes brimming with tears and very obviously distressed, could only murmur, to no one in particular, "What's happened to my boys? What's happened to my boys?" Sergeant Arlie Arneson, one of the waist gunners aboard *T'Ain't A Bird* noted, 'We had taken a beating, a heavy beating. Before the debriefing we received a drink or two of Scotch whiskey instead of coffee and a Spam sandwich. This was a first. All I wanted to do was to go off somewhere quiet to cry or get drunk. I did both'.

On 15 June the 95th Bomb Group moved to Horham nearby and remained there for the duration of the war. Despite the lack of facilities, Framlingham received the 390th Bomb Group on 14 July. This Group, which was commanded by Colonel Edgar M. Wittan, was equipped with B-17F Fortresses that flew in straight from the USA. The 390th became operational on 12 August 1943 and went on to fly 300 missions from Framlingham, the last on 20 April 1945.

B-17Fs in the 570th Bomb Squadron, escorted by high-flying P-47s leaving contrails, en route to Emden on 27 September 1943. They were photographed by Staff Sergeant Stan Smith, a waist gunner in B-17F-120-BO 42-30783 *Stork Club* flown by Captain Keith Harris. In the foreground is B-17F-45-DL 42-3329 *Skippy*, whose pilot, 2nd Lieutenant George W. Harmon, was first to complete twenty-five missions in November 1943. *Stork Club* and 2nd Lieutenant Vincent F. DeMayo's crew FTR on 15 March 1943. On 5 February 1944 *Skippy* took off for a mission to bomb an airfield at Villacoublay, France but whilst departing England the No. 2 engine exploded. Lieutenant Thomas J. Sutters, the pilot was unable to feather the windmilling prop and he decided to return to base but the engine set the wing on fire. They only made it as far as the River Thames where Sutters pointed the B-17 towards the Channel before all ten crew baled out safely. *(USAF)*

Probably the Group's worst mission was on 10 October 1943 to Münster when the 13th Wing lost twenty-five of the thirty B-17s shot down with the 390th Bomb Group losing eight of its eighteen aircraft in about 25 minutes. Captain Robert D. Brown, pilot of *Cabin In The Sky*, asked his tail gunner how the rest of the squadron was doing. The tail gunner reported back that their bomber was the only aircraft left in the squadron formation! Five of the group's eight losses had gone down in as many minutes. A few seconds later Brown saw thirty-six fighters just ahead. His gunners had virtually no ammunition left and the ball-turret gunner could only point his empty guns in the direction of the *Luftwaffe* attacks. But *Cabin In the Sky* came through the

B-17F-100-BO 42-30338 *Cabin in The Sky* in the 571st Bomb Squadron that returned from the raid on Münster on 10 October and Captain Robert Brown put in his gunners' claims of eleven fighters shot down. *Cabin in The Sky* was named from the Broadway musical, which featured the hit song, 'Taking a chance on love'. *(TAMM)*

battle over Münster. Gus Mencow, lead navigator, 520th Bomb Squadron, recalled later:

> This was the most frightening of all the missions I flew. I still get scared and have weird dreams about that day. We did not have complete air supremacy and our fighters did not yet have long-range belly tanks. They could not follow us on long-range missions. We lost eight out of nineteen aircraft. The flak was unbelievable and the *Luftwaffe* must have had every one of their planes attacking us. The loss of so many friends was overwhelming. I got a 109 and it went down smoking and burning.

A live rocket entered the waist window of *Norma J* piloted by Bruce R. Riley, but it did not explode. George T. Rankin grabbed the smouldering projectile in a flak vest and threw it back out of the window. Up front, James H. Shields, one of the few

B-17F-60-DL 42-3426 *Kemy II* in the 571st Bomb Squadron and Lieutenant William W. Smith's crew was one of eight in the 390th Bomb Group, which FTR from Münster on 10 October 1943. Three of the crew were KIA; the other seven survived to be taken prisoner. *(via Ian McLachlan)*

non-commissioned bombardiers in the 8th Air Force, placed his bombs on the target. During the bomb run Lieutenant Burgess W. Murdock, co-pilot of *Miss Carry* in the 390th formation took over the controls. Before the IP a large piece of flak had torn a ragged hole in the thigh of the pilot, Lieutenant Paul W. Vance. Vance used the rubber extension cord from his intercom connection as a tourniquet and wrapped his white flying scarf around the wound. He managed to direct Murdock through the bombing run and helped him maintain formation during the withdrawal from the target area. *Miss Carry* was fortunate. During the bomb run four ships on her wing had fallen out of formation and had been lost. After the target *Tech Supply*, flown by Lieutenant John G. Winant, Jnr., son of the US Ambassador to Great Britain was hit by a rocket and exploded. It was Winant's thirteenthth mission. Winant was among the six men who were taken prisoner. It was a great relief to one and all when the white vapour trails of the Thunderbolt escort could be seen directly ahead. The 390th now comprised a pitiful ten bombers and even the survivors were not sure they would make England. *Rusty Lode*, flown by Lieutenant Robert W. Sabel, had over 750 holes in the fuselage, huge gaps in both wings, rudder and left aileron and both flaps shot away. The bomber had been hit badly before the target but Sabel forced his way home through incessant fighter attacks. Sabel's ball gunner, saw three parachutes open below the aircraft. He knew they must have come from his aircraft so he climbed out of the turret and saw both waist guns hanging limp with their gunners gone. The tail gunner had also left the aircraft. Ellet almost ran to the radio room where he found the radio operator slumped over his gun with what looked like a 20mm cannon shell burst in his face. Ellet scrambled back to the waist

B-17G-5-BO 42-31134 in the 569th Bomb Squadron, en route to the secret German heavy-water plant situated near the little Norwegian town of Rjukan, about 75 miles from Oslo on 16 November 1943. In May 1944, 42-31134 was renamed *Gung Ho* and on 10 September 1944 this aircraft and Lieutenant Charles F. McIntosh's crew FTR from a mission when it crashed at Nuremberg. Six crew were killed and three were taken prisoner. *(USAF)*

door and saw a bloodstained flak suit on the floor. Then the two turret guns opened up and he knew he was not alone after all! Sabel managed to land *Rusty Lode* at Thorpe Abbotts with only two minutes fuel supply remaining. Engineering officers declared that the feat was nothing short of a miracle!

At Framlingham, *Miss Carry* landed at the third attempt in fog. Vance, his leg shattered by a cannon shell, remained in a propped-up position behind the pilot's seat directing Murdock and the top-turret gunner to the airfield. Also at Framlingham, Lieutenant Riley brought *Norma J* in with two engines out and a wounded tail gunner, whose injuries had prevented the crew from baling out. Riley put down in thick fog in a 'field or nothing try' and landed safely.

Bill Cabral and Richard Perry arrived over Framlingham and decided to climb to 2,000ft to give the crew of *The Eightball* a chance to bale out if the rapidly diminishing fuel supply cut out altogether. Framlingham was completely fogged in so Cabral headed for Thorpe Abbotts where the weather was better. He and Perry brought *The Eightball* in for a crash-landing without injury to the crew.

Despite the fog, all ten surviving aircraft in the 390th made it back to Suffolk. *Betty Boop – The Pistol Packin' Mama*, flown by Captain James R. Geary; *Rose Marie* and *Shatzi*, flown by Harold Schuyler, all managed to put down safely. *Cabin In The Sky* also put down without incident and Captain Robert Brown put in his gunners' claims of eleven fighters shot down. Lieutenant Robert Schneider, who was flying *Little Mike* because his regular B-17, *Geronimo*, was undergoing repairs, crash-landed at RAF Wattisham in Suffolk.

On 26 August 956 bombers escorted by 897 fighters attacked targets in France, Belgium, Holland and Germany. Thirteen bombers and thirteen fighters were lost and 148 bombers and fifteen fighters were damaged. Soon after take-off from Framlingham, *Ding Dong Daddy* flown by 1st Lieutenant George E. Smith and 42-102936 in the 390th Bomb Group collided over Hertfordshire near Hitchin and exploded scattering pieces of aeroplane over a two and a half mile area. Everyone aboard *Ding Dong Daddy*, which crashed into woodland minus a wing and without its tail section, was killed while five of the crew of 42-102936, which exploded in mid air, including the pilot, 2nd Lieutenant Paul

H. Bellamy, died. One of the crew on Bellamy's plane had managed to bale out safely but as he was gathering up his parachute, a jagged piece of metal fell from the plane and pierced his chest, killing him instantly. 2nd Lieutenant Raymond A. Klausing, the navigator, survived after being blown clean through the Plexiglas nose.

The 390th Bomb Group took part in the last 8th Air Force shuttle mission on 18 September when 110 B-17s escorted by 150 Mustangs dropped supplies to the Polish Home Army in the ruins of Warsaw.

Framlingham airfield saw some enemy intruder activity on the night of 11/12 April when ten Me 410 intruders of II/KG51 *Edelweiss* attacked over East Anglia. B-17G 42-97556 a PFF ship in the 413th Bomb Squadron, 96th Bomb Group flown by Lieutenant Donald M. MacGregor was coming in to land at Parham at 2200

B-17G-1-BO 42-31122 *Six Nights in Telergma* in the 568th Bomb Squadron, which was the lead ship piloted by Captain Hiram C. Skogmo when it was lost on 11 December 1943 on the mission to Emden. Of the eleven on board only three men survived. Among those lost was Major Ralph V. Hansell, the 390th Bomb Group Operations Officer and strike leader who was flying in the co-pilot's seat. *(TAMM)*

to attend the 390th Bomb Group briefing for a planned raid on Leipzig when it was shot down. The Fortress crashed in the grounds of Glemham House on the Earl of Cranbrook's estate demolishing a section of boundary wall but missing dwellings

B-17F-95-BO 42-30289 *The Dull Tool* (formerly *The Douche Bag*) in the 568th Bomb Squadron, which FTR on 4 January 1944. Four of 2nd Lieutenant James H. Prophett's crew were KIA and six were taken prisoner. *(TAMM)*

B-17F-45-DL-42-3329/F *Skippy* in the 570th Bomb Squadron taxies out at Framlingham with other Fortresses. *Skippy* was salvaged on 8 February 1944. *(USAF)*

and the church. MacGregor and eight of the crew suffered serious injuries and three men were killed. On 27 December 1944 during freezing conditions, a tragic accident occurred when, at 0840 a bomb-laden Fortress (42-107010 *Gloria Ann II* flown by Flight Officer James E. McGuire) crashed shortly after take-off from the E–W runway. *Gloria Ann II* rose to 50ft but it is believed that icing caused the Fortress gradually to lose height, following the fall of the countryside, before hitting a roadside bank

B-17G-70-DL 44-6954 dropping supplied to the Dutch during the series of six 'Chowhound' mercy missions, which ended on 7 May. During the winter of 1944–45 15,000 Dutch civilians died of starvation.
(via Truett Woodall)

The Dutch show their gratitude for the supply drops by cutting the words 'THANK YOU BOYS' out of flowers growing in bulb fields and the words, 'MANY THANKS' could be seen from the air in other fields. *(via Truett Woodall)*

and exploding in the village street at Parham destroying the chapel. All nine crew were killed and most houses in the vicinity damaged, but no civilians were injured. A local reporter said that 'the village resembled a battlefield'.

On Sunday 14 January 1945 the 8th Air Force dispatched over 650 bombers supported by fifteen fighter groups to mainly oil and other targets in central and north-western Germany again. The *Luftwaffe* jumped the 390th and in about a 3-minute fight shot down all eight of the low squadron which was lagging 2,000ft below and behind the rest of the group because of supercharger

B-17G in the 569th Bomb Squadron at Framlingham. *(USAF)*

Once victory in Europe was finally secured, the bomb groups were hastily re-tasked as transports and pressed into service shuffling former Allied PoWs home and airlifting displaced people from all over Europe. They also transported troops from the UK to Casablanca, where they continued on to the CBI (China-Burma-India) Theatre, and helped move fighter groups to bases in Germany. Pictured is B-17G-40-DL 44-6097/D in the 390th Bomb Group. *(TAMM)*

Wartime hut at Parham in the 1980s. *(Author)*

Parham airfield in June 2006. (*Author*)

problems with the leading B-17. Then they hit the 390th high squadron and four B-17s went down.

The 390th Bomb Group left Framlingham in August 1945 to return to the USA. The airfield was then in charge of an RAF holding party but was never used by any other flying units and it became instead a clearing station for the rehabilitation of Polish nationals before being abandoned. Mr. Percy Kindred of Crabbs

Members of a vehicle re-enactment group at Parham in July 2007. (*Author*)

B-17G *Sally B* as she flies over the Parham tower in July 2007. *(Author)*

Farm leased back his land, which formed the majority of the airfield, before this was finally sold back to him in 1963–1964. The runways had to be broken up and removed by the St. Ives Sand & Gravel for agricultural reasons but the perimeter track was retained as a runway for aircraft. Many of the original camp buildings remained intact and the Ministry of Environment retained the single T2 hangar.

Ladies wearing WWII clothes wave to B-17G *Sally B* as she flies over the Parham tower in July 2007. *(Author)*

Great Ashfield – Station 155

The airfield was built in 1942 by John Laing & Son Ltd to the standard Class 'A' airfield specification, although the NW–SE runway was 100 yards longer than the usual 1,400 yards. Seventeen 'spectacle' loop concrete hardstandings were added to the original planned thirty-three 'frying-pan' types before completion of the field to allow a whole USAAF group to be accommodated. The technical site was on the south side of the perimeter track and the temporary buildings of the camp were also dispersed to the south. During the construction of the flying field, 3,000 trees and eight miles of hedge were uprooted, while the volume of excavation ran to 250,000 cubic yards. Altogether, some 108,000 cubic yards of concrete was used and ballast obtained locally amounted to 250,000 tons.

The first aircraft to land on the station is believed to have been a battle-damaged B-26 Marauder returning from a raid over Holland on 17 May 1943. On 19 June the members of the 385th Bomb Group or 'Van's Valiants', as they were called after their first Commanding Officer, Colonel Elliott Vandevanter, arrived, their B-17 Fortress aircraft following five days later. The 385th was assigned to the 4th Bomb Wing, which controlled the other Suffolk B-17 bases and flew its first combat mission on 17 July. Exactly a month later, when the group was participating in the only direct England–Africa shuttle mission, the base was officially handed over from the RAF to the USAAF. On 29 July 1943 when eighty-one Fortresses in the 4th Wing attacked the Heinkel assembly plant at Warnemünde the 385th Bomb Group lost three B-17s in a mid-air collision during assembly at only 2,000ft, two miles from the English coast. Only six parachutes were seen to leave the three aircraft. However, the bombing of the Heinkel plant was described as excellent and Fw 190 production was severely curtailed.

On the Schweinfurt mission on 17 August the 385th Bomb Group lost three bombers. On 9 October 378 B-17s and B-24s were dispatched to three targets in East Prussia and Poland in the longest mission to date. As previously described, the third force of B-17s, which bombed Marienburg, achieved the greatest success of the day. The normally unfortunate 385th Bomb Group led the raid and lost only two aircraft, one through engine trouble. A lack of anti-aircraft defences, thought unnecessary at a target so far from England, meant that the force could bomb from between 11,000 and 13,000ft with excellent results and the plant, which had been producing almost 50 per cent of the *Luftwaffe*'s Fw 190s was devastated.

Frank Walls in the co-pilot's window of *Shack Bunny*, 551st Bomb Squadron. This B-17F and Lieutenant Lyle V. Fryer's crew were lost over France on 20 October 1943 on the mission to Duren, Germany. All the crew were taken prisoner. *(William Nicholls)*

No. 1 hangar, one of two T2s built, was badly damaged on 3 September 1943, when a bombed-up B-17 standing nearby caught fire and exploded. Then on the night of 22/23 May 1944, a German intruder scored a direct hit with one of the seven bombs dropped and the airfield was strafed.

On 6 March 1944 when 730 B-17s and B-24s were dispatched to targets in the suburbs of Berlin it proved the most costly mission the Eighth ever flew. The 3rd Division, which was assigned the Robert Bosch Electrical Equipment factory, was led by the 4th Combat Bombardment Wing commander, Brigadier General Russell Wilson, who took off from Great Ashfield in *Chopstick G-George*, a PFF ship in the 812th Bomb Squadron, 482nd Bomb Group, equipped with H_2X radar. It was flown by Major Fred A. Rabbo with a mixed 385th Bomb Group and 482nd Bomb Group crew which included 1st Lieutenant John C. 'Red' Morgan who received the Medal of Honor for his actions on 26 July 1943. All the 385th aircraft returned safely though Wilson's B-17 was

1st Lieutenant John C. Morgan MoH (Medal of Honor) ladles out soup in *Stalag Luft III* at Sagan in Silesia. Morgan was shot down on the mission to Berlin on 6 March 1944 flying from Great Ashfield in *Chopstick G-George* in the 812th Bomb Squadron, 482nd Bomb Group flown by Major Fred A. Rabbo. *(USAF)*

hit by flak and exploded, killing eight of the crew instantly and catapulting Morgan, who was carrying a back-pack parachute under his arm, out of the aircraft. He managed to put it on after several attempts and was saved from possible injury when a tree broke his fall.

On 11 April 830 bombers were dispatched in three separate forces to bomb aircraft production centres in eastern Germany. The 13th and 45th Combat Wings in the 3rd Bomb Division force were also confronted with bad weather in the Poznan area and were forced to bomb the secondary target at Rostock. Rocket-firing Me 410s and Ju88s took advantage of a lapse in fighter cover and wreaked havoc among the leading groups. The 96th Bomb Group was worst hit, losing ten of the twenty-five bombers lost this day. Most of the crews who got back to England had been in the air for more than 11 hours and tiredness had already begun to take effect during the last stages of the homeward leg. Lieutenant Bryce S. Moore, pilot of B-17 *Esky* (after the trademark character on the front of *Esquire* magazine) in the 551st or 'Green' Squadron, returned from Stettin, his 26th and next to last mission and longest at 10 hours and 30 minutes. He recalls:

I was terribly distraught that the group lead radioed in the clear that because of weather we would bypass Stettin and bomb an alternate target. I knew the Germans monitored our frequencies and to alert their defences of our imminent arrival seemed sheer stupidity at the moment, though I don't recall actually encountering any enemy fighter attacks or anti-aircraft fire over the target, whatever its name. On reflection I suspect that Colonel Vandevanter, the Command Pilot, was using a code name to mislead the enemy. If so, it worked. We were flying left wing (low) in the second element in the low squadron; not a good position because of the stratus clouds the group was struggling to climb over at about 28,000 or 30,000ft. Being the lowest ship in the group we were dragged through the tops of several cloud layers made worse by dense contrails from the planes ahead and above us and by other groups ahead of us whose contrails were some-times at right angles to our heading as they climbed. This created a false sloping horizon and making us feel we were in a turn when we weren't. Very uncomfortable, near-vertigo

Cartoon from Army Talk 1944. B-17 42-32078 *Barbara Bee* in the 550th Bomb Squadron survived the war and was scrapped at Kingman, Arizona.

intermittently for a few seconds. To avoid running into other planes in the clouds I pulled to the left for 10 or 15 seconds then continued to climb straight ahead with all aboard keeping a lookout for other aircraft. Suddenly I noticed a small break in the cloud layer below us to my left and was surprised to see for perhaps two seconds a squadron of six twin-engine German fighter-bombers about 500ft below heading in the opposite direction. Apparently they were unaware of our presence, though of course I couldn't be certain. I called out their location to the crew and told the co-pilot that if the German squadron should attack our lone airplane we would dodge them by re-entering the cloud layer a few feet below. I then called the navigator and suggested he tune nearby Malmo, Sweden, on the radio compass in case we needed a safe haven from the German fighters since the clouds seemed thickest to our right (north). "It's been tuned for five minutes!" was the quick reply. Happily, the Germans didn't attack and in a few minutes we were between cloud layers, sighted the group a short distance ahead, quickly caught up and proceeded to the new target. The trip home was uneventful till letdown when we broke up into squadrons

and widened our disassembly pattern because of hazy conditions over East Anglia. Suddenly our squadron met another
squadron head-on, with no time to manoeuvre. How we
missed each other will forever be a mystery.

On 18 April nine crews in the 385th failed to return from
the mission to Berlin. On 29 April 768 bomber crews throughout
East Anglia were awakened early for briefing. At Great Ashfield
Carlyle J. Hanson was one who made the mission. Hanson recalls:

We got up at 0130 for target 'Study'. The target was Berlin!
The assembly was rough because the overcast went up to
12,000ft. We were the lead ship in the high squadron of the
lead group. After a messy wing assembly, the lead pathfinder
went out in the middle of the Channel and the second one
took over. It seemed like we got flak all the way in. Everything was covered with clouds.

B-17G-50-DL 44-6483 in the 550th Bomb Squadron was named *Ruby's
Raiders* by Lieutenant Blackwell's crew after Ruby Newell, a WAC named
by Yank magazine as the most beautiful WAC in the ETO. She was
present at Great Ashfield when the nose art by Corporal Ploss was
dedicated. *Ruby's Raiders* finished her days at Kingman, Arizona in
November 1945. *(USAF)*

Part of the 4th Combat Wing had strayed off course and near Magdeburg the enemy fighters wreaked havoc among the un-protected formation: shooting down or fatally damaging eighteen Fortresses in 20 minutes. Seven of them came from the 385th Bomb Group. Technical Sergeant Clarence L. Mossman, left waist-gunner in the *Worry Bird*, flown by 28 year old Cleveland, Ohio pilot, Lieutenant Richard A. Spencer in the 549th Bomb Squadron, recalls:

> We were flying a tight formation and all the squadrons seemed to be in their right positions when the German fighters attacked. We did evasive action to help us from head-on attacks. We first spotted about 200 fighters about 12 o'clock high and in a few minutes they attacked us head-on, coming down out of the sun in waves of forty and sixty at a time, and doing barrel rolls right through the formations. They made three passes. Our left and also our right wingman went down. We had a lot of flak damage on our aircraft and also damage to our wing from 20mm shells fired by Me 109s that came down through our formation. All of the crew came through the mission without being wounded or killed.

On 6 October, when the 8th went to Berlin at the IP near Nauen the 3rd Division formation was forced to lose altitude to

prevent flying through thick cloud. Unknown to the B-17 crews, in this layer of cloud lurked a strong force of enemy fighters. Using the cloud cover to excellent advantage, the German fighters were vectored by ground controllers right into the 385th Bomb Group formation, flying as the high group of the last combat wing. The surprise was total. To make matters worse, the 549th Bomb Squadron was in the process of turning on to the

Great Ashfield village sign. *(Author)*

Great Ashfield airfield in June 2006. *(Author)*

target and had become separated from the rest of the group. Most of the eleven B-17s shot down were from this squadron. Only the arrival of the P-51 escort prevented further carnage.

The 385th flew 296 missions from Great Ashfield and lost 129 B-17s. *Satan's Mate* earned itself distinction as being 'the Fort that looped'. It was on 19 February 1945 during the return flight from a mission to Germany, that Lieutenant James Fleisher began to climb to avoid flying in cloud. As he did so, the Fortress crossed the slipstream of another unseen aircraft causing the aircraft to fall over backwards, the crew being pinned to the sides in a 380mph power dive. On their return to Great Ashfield, the aircraft was found to have stripped seventy-four rivets and strained the tailplane. The group returned to the USA in July 1945, the last element leaving the base on 4 August. After the airfield reverted to RAF control in October 1945, it came under Maintenance Command as an MU site and sub-site for bomb storage before being finally abandoned and sold in 1959–60. It has now been returned to agricultural use by the Miles family of Norton Hall.

8

Honington – Station 375

Honington was in use by Eighth Air Force units for a longer period than any other airfield in this country; albeit principally as a maintenance base. Honington was turned over to the USAAF in the summer of 1942 and it became an air depot for the major overhaul of aircraft, later specializing in B-17 models and supporting the 3rd Bomb Division located in the area. A special depot, with full technical facilities for this work, was established on an adjacent site known as Troston and the organisation functioning in this logistic role was known as the 1st Strategic Air Depot. Badly damaged Fortresses were often instructed to crash land at Honington on return from operations, particularly if their landing gear could not be lowered, as this avoided the necessity to dismantle and transport the aircraft from its home base for repair!

A steel mat runway, 2,000 yards by 40 yards was laid during the American occupation along an E–W axis. An extensive system of taxiways with seventy-five hardstandings was also developed during this period and an additional nine blister hangars were located at various points around the airfield. The construction of the Troston depot involved additional taxiways and hardstandings and the erection of more hangars and buildings. This site was to the north-west of the airfield. Honington also housed an operational fighter unit, the 364th, from February 1944, the Group utilising hardstandings and blister hangars on the opposite side

B-17Gs under repair at the US depot at RAF Honington in 1944. Nearest aircraft is 42-37972 *Gold Brick* XR-H in the 349th Bomb Squadron, 100th Bomb Group with most of the left wing missing. This was the result of a mishap on the morning of 30 January 1944 when Lieutenant James R. Stout took off from Thorpe Abbotts for Brunswick and had to feather No. 1 engine but as he prepared to land he found that the landing gear was inoperative. He circled the field to use up gas, jettisoned bombs and ball turret in the Channel and crashed at Honington. *Gold Brick* resumed combat missions but needed further work when it returned to Thorpe Abbotts with its right stabilizer missing as a result of a *Rammjäger* attack on a mission on 7 April 1945. Next is 42-31100 *The Gimp* in the 709th Bomb Squadron, 447th Bomb Group. Behind is 42-37716 BX-P in the 338th Bomb Squadron, 96th Bomb Group. *(USAF via Philip Kaplan)*

of the airfield to the air depot. On 28 February the CO, Lieutenant Colonel Frederick C. Grambo, accompanying a 20th Fighter Group mission to gain operational experience, crashed near Zwolle in Holland and was killed.

The first of 342 missions by the 364th began on 3 March 1944 and the unit was awarded a Distinguished Unit Citation for defence of bombers over Frankfurt on 27 December. The Group operated P-38 Lightnings until July 1944 when it converted to P-51 Mustangs. Although the last mission by the 364th took place on 25 April 1945, the group did not depart until November. Even then, Honington remained a lone Eighth Air Force outpost in the UK becoming Fighter Command HQ in October 1945.

Honington airfield in August 2006. *(Author)*

By the beginning of 1946, Honington remained the only active station of all the 122 which had been occupied by the Eighth Air Force and a fitting ceremony was planned to mark its closure and official handing back to the Royal Air Force. On 26 February Brigadier General Emil Kiel, the Eighth Fighter Command commander, was present to hand over the keys of the station to Air Marshal Sir James Robb, AOC RAF Fighter Command. An RAF band played 'The Star-Spangled Banner' as the Stars and Stripes were lowered for the RAF Ensign to be hoisted in its place. Unfortunately bad weather prevented the final Eighth Air Force B-17 Fortress mission over Britain in which it was intended that 44-83273 was to take off with General Kiel as a last farewell gesture. When the last American personnel left Honington in March, the airfield reverted to the RAF, the first occupants being the Transport Command Aircraft Modification Unit.

9

Horham – Station 119

Horham was one of the earliest of the new heavy bomber
bases built in East Suffolk to be opened, although at first
it was intended for use by the RAF. With 2,000-yard and
1,400-yard bomber runways, Horham was originally planned with
thirty dispersals but these were increased in number during
construction to bring the airfield up to US bomber requirements.
The two early T2 hangars erected on the south side of the airfield
were painted in black and dark earth shadow shading camouflage
in contrast to later airfields in the district where the hangars
were finished in tar varnish. The technical site was adjacent to the
two hangers beside the B1117 road to Eye. Station headquarters,
administrative buildings and dispersed living sites were temporary constructions chiefly of the Nissen hut type and dispersed
in farmland to the west of the airfield in the parish of Denham.

Horham received its first American air units on 5 October
1942 when the 47th Bomb Group began arriving from Bury St.
Edmunds with fifty A-20B Havocs. The Group was scheduled to
join the Twelfth Air Force in North Africa and the aircraft and
men left Horham between November and January 1943. A B-26C
Marauder unit was the next to take up residence, the 323rd Group
arriving in May 1943 but moving on to Earls Colne after less than
a month at Horham. Its place was taken immediately (15 June) by
the 95th Bomb Group, a B-17F unit which was previously based at
Framlingham; the move being made because of the incomplete

Lieutenant Robert P. Bender in the 336th Bomb Squadron. On 12 May 1943
B-17F-65-BO 42-29704 *Spook* suffered bomb damage in the mission to Lorient but the
Fortress made it back. On 17 May Bender crash-landed *Spook* at RAF Exeter
returning from a mission to the U-boat pens in France and it was so badly shot up
that it was salvaged. (*Spook II* joined the 379th Bomb Group on 22 June and was
renamed *Lady Astrid*. It went MIA with Lieutenant Johnson's crew on the 14 October
1943 mission to Schweinfurt. *Spook III* was lost on 28 July with 2nd Lieutenant
Francis J. Regan's crew when they ditched in the North Sea). On 28 June, low on fuel
and with an engine shot out over St. Nazaire, 60 miles from England Bender ditched
Spook IV in the Channel. The crew was finally rescued by ASR 22 hours later. On a
subsequent visit to a cinema the combat-fatigued pilot went berserk when a
newsreel showed Fw 190s attacking B-17s. Then on a test flight take-off in *Spook V*,
Bender froze at the stick. Don Merton the co-pilot overpowered him and prevented a
crash. Bender never flew *Spook V* again (nor *Spook VI* that followed it in November
1943). He was hospitalized and returned to America, where he died of a heart attack
at the age of 25. On 29 January 1944 *Spook V* crashed on the mission on 29 January
1944 with the loss of five of 2nd Lieutenant James D. Higgins' crew. Five men
survived to be taken prisoner. (*USAF*)

state and lack of facilities at the latter airfield. Colonel Alfred A. Kessler, who had been CO of the 95th Bomb Group since October 1942, was moved out on 22 June and Colonel John Gerhart, who had been one of the 8th's original staff officers at its activation in January 1942, took over.

On 28 June the 95th Bomb Group lost three B-17s to enemy action. On 10 July when ten B-17s of the 4th Bomb Wing went to Le Bourget airfield, *Exterminator*, a 412th Bomb Squadron Fortress flown by Lieutenant James R. Sarchet, was shot down by *Leutnant* Helmut Hoppe CO 4th Staffel, JG 26 near Fecamp, west of Rouen in his first pass.

On 24 January 1944 857 bomber crews were briefed to attack aviation industry plants and marshalling yards at Frankfurt. Two B-17s were lost in action and both were from the 335th Bomb

Smoke trails from B-17F-100-BO 42-30377 *Roger The Lodger II* in the 412th Bomb Squadron, shortly before it went down in flames in Dutch territorial waters with Lieutenant Ralph W. Eherts' crew on the Marienburg mission, 9 October 1943. Fighters scored hits in the No. 2 engine aboard *Roger The Lodger II* and put a rocket in the No. 3 engine. Seven of Ehert's crew baled out but two of the parachutes were on fire. The five survivors perished in the freezing waters of the North Sea. Robert Wing the bombardier had a premonition the night before that he would not return. *(USAF)*

B-17G-10-BO 42-31329 in the 334th Bomb Squadron, which crash landed
at Oberriet-Kriessern, Switzerland on the mission to Augsburg on
16 March 1944. Five of Lieutenant James W. Reed's crew were interned
and five who baled out over Germany were taken prisoner.
(via Hans Heiri Stapfer)

Squadron. *Feldwebel* Kurt Schmidtke of the 4th Staffel JG 26
claimed a B-17 at Calais and it was confirmed. 42-30181, *Lover
Boy* piloted by 2nd Lieutenant Clay A. Burnett was shot down
at Brussels with the loss of four men KIA. Six men survived
and were taken prisoner. 42-37756 *Roarin Bill* flown by 2nd
Lieutenant Charles H. Mowers went down at Waterloo (three
evaded, one KIA, six PoW).

The 95th Bomb Group went on to complete 320 missions
receiving three Distinguished Unit Citations for Regensburg,
17 August 1943, Münster, 10 October 1943 and Berlin, 4 March
1944. Aircraft on the 4 March 1944 mission were recalled because
of weather conditions but two squadrons from the 95th (and one
from the 100th) failed to intercept the signal. By carrying on to the
target, the 95th became the first American unit to bomb Berlin,
losing four Fortresses in the process. Those aircraft that did get
through to the capital claimed to have dropped the first American
bombs on Berlin. The formation, led by the 95th Bomb Group
went for a visual run but the clouds closed in again and at 1342
hours the bombs were released under the direction of the leading
482nd Bomb Group PFF aircraft flown by Lieutenant William
Owens, by which time flak had eased off. The return journey was
'nothing short of a nightmare' and mostly was flown through
'solid layers of clouds' as the formation was forced to descend
because of diminishing oxygen supplies. On landing at Horham

B-17G-15-DL 42-37889 *Pride of Chehalis*, 336th Bomb Squadron, being inspected by locals after crashing in a potato field near Vroomshoop, the Netherlands on 29 June 1944. 1st Lieutenant J. D. Cook and his crew baled out safely before the Fortress went down. Two men evaded capture. *(Coen Cornelissen)*

and Thorpe Abbotts the exhausted B-17 crews were given a rapturous welcome by their ground crews and within minutes all of them were enveloped by the triumphant ground staff and toasted with a general issue of double scotches. The 95th Bomb Group was unique in the 8th Air Force, being awarded its third Presidential Unit Citation.

At Horham on D-Day, 6 June 1944, Henry Tarcza, a B-17 engineer-gunner in Mathew McEntee's crew, was awakened some hours before daylight. At first he thought that this was just another routine bombing mission over enemy-occupied Europe. Shortly after 0300 hours he enjoyed a breakfast of bacon and country fresh eggs, a wartime delicacy reserved only for the combat flying personnel. They entered the maximum security briefing room around 0400 hours where the huge map on the wall was covered with yards of thick drapery. After all the noise of shifting chairs had ceased the briefing officer calmly pulled the covering material toward him and a long moan from all the flying men echoed throughout the room, followed by a hoarse whisper, 'Invasion'. McEntee's crew said little as they proceeded to their bomber *El's Bells*, named by McEntee in honour of his girlfriend

B-17G-80-BO 43-38229 *Better Duck* in the 334th Bomb Squadron, survived the war and was broken up for scrap at Kingman, Arizona in December 1945. *(USAF)*

B-17G-10-DL 42-37756 *Roarin Bill* in the 335th Bomb Squadron that was lost with 2nd Lieutenant Charles H. Mowers' crew on 24 January 1944 when it crashed at Waterloo, Belgium. Three crew evaded, one was KIA and six were taken prisoner. The replacement *Roarin Bill* in the 335th Bomb Squadron (B-17G-20-BO 42-31462) force landed on the Continent on 20 January 1945. Seven in Captain F. Beard's crew returned and two were taken prisoner. *(via TAMM)*

B-17F-95-BO 42-30235 The *Zoot Suiters* (formerly *Lonesome Polecat*) which was assigned overseas on 16 June 1943 when it was allocated to the 91st Bomb Group. It later transferred to the 412th Bomb Squadron, 95th Bomb Group and in October 1945 was scrapped at Altus, Oklahoma. *(via Michael Faley)*

Former Mess hall doors near the Red Feather Club in the 1970s. *(Author)*

Sergeants & Airmen's ablutions Drying Room at Horham. *(Author)*

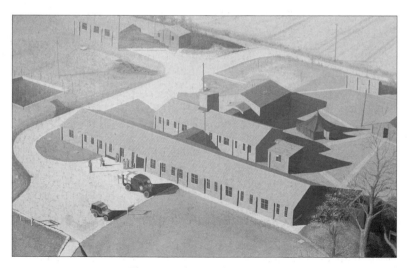

The Base Hospital in WWII.

Air raid shelter near the Hospital site with wartime graffiti. *(Author)*

Outline drawing scratched with a stone in an air raid shelter at Horham. *(Author)*

Suffolk Forever scratched with a stone in an air raid shelter at Horham. *(Author)*

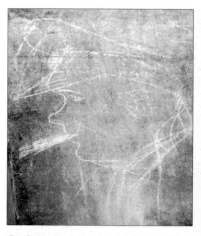

Outline drawings scratched with a stone in an air raid shelter at Horham. *(Author)*

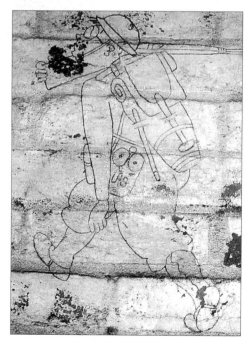

Wall art at Horham in the 1980s. *(Author)*

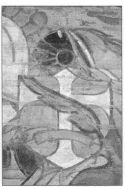

Red Feather Club murals by Nathan Bindler. (*Author*)

Red Feather Club murals by Nathan Bindler. (*Author*)

in New York City and whom he later married, in a canvas-covered truck. Tarcza was sure they all felt as he did. If the Germans shared his secret at that moment it could alter the destiny of mankind. They all did a good job of maintaining composure so that the ground crews might not suspect that D-Day had, in fact, arrived. The air was thick with eastbound aircraft for as many miles as he could see in all directions. *El's Bells* joined in and headed toward France. McEntee gazed with awe at the hundreds of ships and boats off Omaha Beach. It appeared from his altitude that 'one could almost step from one vessel to another and walk between England and France'. The Group encountered no German aircraft in the target area and enemy gunfire was very light and

Windswept and waterlogged runway at Horham. (*Author*)

Horham airfield. *(Author)*

inaccurate. Back at Horham the crew of *El's Bells* were interviewed by the press. Emotions varied: many of their thoughts, feelings and opinions they kept to themselves. Mathew McEntee, said, "Thank you men for your fine co-operation as a combat crew. It is doubtful if any of us will ever in our lifetime, participate in a historic undertaking of this magnitude". So far nobody has.

The 95th remained at Horham until the end of hostilities when the group was redeployed to the USA during June–August 1945. When the group departed, it gave its Stars and Stripes head-quarters' flag to the nearby Stradbroke church where it can still be seen today. The airfield was returned to the RAF on 9 October 1945 and became a satellite for Nos 25 and 262 Maintenance Units. The hangars were dismantled and it was declared a surplus inactive station in October 1948. In later years, an RAF Blood-hound missile site used one part of the airfield but when this was moved, the complete site was sold during the years 1961–64. A mushroom growing plant was established at the end of one runway during the 1960s, but the work of the St. Ives Sand & Gravel Company is evident elsewhere. However, located on the west side, well away from the flying field, the hospital is still in good repair, now being used by the local farmer for grain drying. Inside, the various doors leading to what were the main ward, dental surgeon's office, duty nurse, and other administrative staff departments still bear the stencilled names.

Knettishall – Station 136

T his Class 'A' airfield was constructed by W. & C. French Ltd during 1942–1943 within a triangle formed by the villages of Coney Weston, Hopton and Knettishall. It comprised three intersecting runways, thirty dispersed hardstandings, two T2-type hangars and the usual range of technical and domestic buildings. The last named, mainly Nissen huts, were located on the Coney Weston side of the airfield. David Calcutt, a Coney Weston schoolboy recalls.

> You can imagine the impact it had, around 3,000 men arriving in our small village, all with film star accents and many with suntans. I am only glad I was a small child at the time! Our narrow roads were busy with convoys of supplies and there were many young and so-friendly Yanks who stopped to ask the way. They were very good to the children and we were invited to the camp on special occasions for a party.

> The base was allocated to the Eighth Air Force and on 23 June 1943 advance parties of the 388th Bombardment Group (Heavy) arrived, although some of the construction work had still to be completed. The Group was equipped with B-17F/G Fortresses and was commanded by Colonel William H. David. The Group's four squadrons were the 360th, 361st, 362nd and 363rd. On 17 July

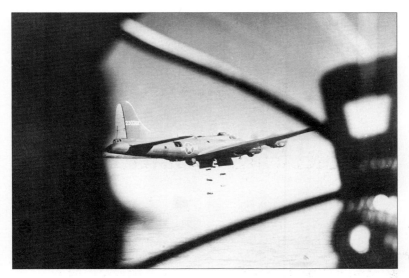

B-17F-100-BO 42-30362 *The Bonnie II* in the 561st Bomb Squadron, releases its bomb load on target. *The Bonnie II* and Lieutenant Adalbert D. Porter's crew FTR on 9 September 1943 when flak and a 20mm shell hit the B-17 on the bomb run over Paris, creating a large hole in the wing near the No. 1 engine. Bombs were jettisoned and the crew baled out, the aircraft crashing at Houilles. Five crew evaded capture; the other six were captured and made prisoners of war. *(USAF)*

when a record 332 bombers were dispatched to Hanover, the 388th Bomb Group (and the 385th) flew their first mission as part of the 4th Wing, which attacked the Fokker plant at Amsterdam. Due to cloud cover, some of the bombs were off target and as a result 130 Dutch civilians were killed. On 24 July, during 'Blitz Week', the Group flew to Norway where the briefed target was Bergen. Again cloud obscured the aiming point and although some of the formation bombed the alternative target at Trondheim, most of the bomb loads were brought back. Two days later the target was Hanover, which was a more successful mission but five of the Group's Fortresses were shot down. One of them was ditched in the sea off Overstrand and the crew were rescued.

The Knettishall Group took part in the Regensburg 'shuttle' raid on 17 August 1943 when the 4th Wing flew on to bases in North Africa after bombing the aircraft plant. In spite of the hard

B-17G-45-BO 42-97328 *Heaven's Above* in the 561st Bomb Squadron, which was assigned overseas on 22 March 1944. It returned to the ZOI (Zone of the Interior – USA) in June 1945 and was scrapped at Kingman, Arizona in December 1945. *(USAF)*

air battles en route, the 388th lost only one of the total of twenty-four Fortresses missing in the 4th Bomb Wing. For their part in this action the Group, along with the other 4th Bomb Wing groups taking part, was awarded a Distinguished Unit Citation. Later that month the first of several visits to V-weapons sites took place when the Group's target was Watten. On 6 September the target was the aircraft component factories at Stuttgart. The 388th Bomb Group was flying its 19th mission, which would be one to remember. At the IP flak had claimed 2nd Lieutenant J. A. Roe's B-17 *Silver Dollar* in the 563rd Squadron and shortly there-after fighters shot down the squadron's five remaining aircraft. 1st Lieutenant W. P. Beecham's crew in *Impatient Virgin II* were interned in Switzerland and *Sky Shy*, flown by Flight Officer M. Bowen, tried to join him but the aircraft was on fire and the tail gunner had been killed in his turret. Nine men baled out and German civilians murdered the radioman. In all, the group lost

B-17G-l00-BO 43-38933/G *Weary Wolf* (formerly *Dear Mom II*) in the 561st
Bomb Squadron, in formation with B-17G-105-BO 43-39221/N, hit a hill
near Lands End on 17 May 1945 during a navigational training exercise.
The pilot, 2nd Lieutenant H. J. Cole, his co-pilot, 2nd Lieutenant
V.Ferguson, two navigators and two groundcrew who flew as engineer
and radio operator were all killed. *(via Robert M. Foose)*

eleven Fortresses, the highest loss it had sustained on a raid since
joining the 8th in June and the Group's highest loss of the war.

From 13 September 1943 the 388th Bomb Group and the 96th
Bomb Group at Snetterton Heath and the 452nd at Deopham
Green formed the 45th Combat Bombardment Wing in the 3rd
Bomb Division. The 388th Bomb Group Fortresses were identified
by an 'H' in a square on the fin, and the drab olive and grey
camouflage gradually gave way to natural metal replacements.
Later in the war two parallel black hands on upper right and lower
left wings and the fin and rudder were painted on the Group's
B-17s. Colonel Chester C. Cox took command of the Group on
7 October 1943 and he remained in control of the Group until just
after the war. The port area at Gdynia in Poland was the target
for 9 October 1943 when among the shipping hit was the liner
Stuttgart. Three days later the Group was part of the task force of
300 Fortresses that went to Schweinfurt, the 388th Bomb Group
losing just one aircraft, which crashed on take-off. Fifteen other
B-17s were damaged in action. Lieutenant Dan Sullivan put *Susie*

B-17G-35-DL 42-107062 *Worry Bird* (formerly *Miss Bea Haven*) in the 562nd Bomb Squadron over Suffolk in 1944. This aircraft was scrapped at Kingman, Arizona in November 1945. *(USAF)*

Sagtits down at Biggin Hill with the gear up, having lost all hydraulic fluid from a flak hit and with no brakes he still managed to avoid the Spitfires parked all around. The plane, whose name, even by 8th Air Force standards, was more than a little risqué, was showing red on all fuel tanks and had been through a lot, as Richard Donner explains:

> After bomb release we lost an engine and started to drop out of formation. Dan Sullivan took a poll as to whether we should go to Switzerland or try to get to France where the girls are prettier. France it was! Problems arose with enemy fighters after leaving the Group. After damaging two Fw 190s our tail gunner was hit. We were able to hold altitude at 5,000ft but the 'Abbeville Kids' were distracting us. Sullivan went down to some low clouds. The next poll was whether we should try to get across the Channel. We got in sight of the chalk cliffs, then unbelievably, the solid cloud cover over England opened up. Beneath was an airstrip. We had lost the hydraulic system along the way, so we cranked down the wheels. *Susie Sagtits* made six or eight ground loops with no

damage. The crew were able to get repairs and fly back to Knettishall after three days.

One of the men who beat the odds was New Yorker Larry Goldstein, who flew a tour of twenty-five missions as a radio operator on B-17s in the 563rd Bomb Squadron, September 1943–March 1944.

With twenty-nine other crews we were assigned to a replacement pool and after five days we were rushed to a bomb group as replacement crews for those lost. When we entered our barracks on a cold dreary night all we saw were empty beds. We were told that these were the beds of men who had been shot down a few days before. A very sobering thought for us as a group. Suddenly flying status was not that appealing. Someone said out loud, "And we volunteered for this?" Each flight became more dangerous as the air war was stepped up. Air Force history has recorded this period as the heaviest of WWII and the most important air raids on Germany were flown. If a crew survived eight to ten missions at this time they were considered lucky. We were able to complete the twenty-five. I guess someone up there was looking out for our crew. Every time that I entered the plane for a mission I never thought that our crew would not return that afternoon. Every flight was an adventure; so many things could go wrong. We had our share, but fortunately none were bad enough to cause any harm to any of the crew. Except on one occasion. We made a forced landing with one engine on fire, a full gas and bomb load but we were able to evacuate the aircraft safely with one exception. Howie Palmer was injured rather severely when he stumbled into a part of the Fortress just after it came to a halt. He never did fly with us again as he was hospitalized for many months. Our twenty-five missions were not simple, each one worse that the last, but when we were briefed on 4 March 1944 for our twenty-fifth and last we had hoped for an easy run and then home to the good old USA but that was not to be the case. The target was the first daylight raid on Berlin. When we came out of the clouds over the English Channel and saw the White Cliffs of Dover it was the most beautiful sight that I could ever hope to see. A few days later, 'BJ' our pilot came into our quarters and ordered us all to accompany him to the base chapel and there we really became one crew that was thankful for completing our missions without a major injury.

Early in 1944 the Group continued its contribution to the strategic offensive against industrial targets and in March they paid their first of several visits to Berlin. In the weeks leading up to the Allied invasion of Europe, the Group was switched to communications and other tactical targets prior to D-Day and for a time after the landings.

As part of Operation Frantic (shuttle missions to Russia), the 388th Bomb Group led the 45th Combat Bombardment Wing in an attack on synthetic oil plant at Ruhland, 30 miles south of Berlin, on 21 June 1944. After a nearly 12-hour flight, the Wing landed at Poltava to the east of Kiev after effectively bombing their target. Four squadrons of Mustangs provided close escort for the latter part of the mission, although enemy aerial opposition turned out to be slight. However, the task force was shadowed to their destination by *Luftwaffe* aircraft and some hours after landing the airfield at Poltava was devastated by about sixty Heinkel He111s and Junkers Ju88s. Ammunition and fuel dumps were hit and forty-four Fortresses were wrecked and most of the others badly

Gunners Briefing Room which once graced the airfield. *(Author)*

Gunners Briefing Room. *(Author)*

damaged, making this a very costly mission in materiel although few casualties in American personnel resulted. On 12 May the first major attacks were made on oil installations and for its part in the attack on Brüx, coupled with their effort on the Russian shuttle mission, the 388th Bomb Group was awarded a second DUC.

Dedication ceremony for the 388th Bomb group Memorial on 17 May 1986. *(Author)*

Wall art at Knettishall in the 1970s, some of which were painted after the war. (*Author*)

Wall art at Knettishall. *(Author)*

On 24 December 1944 the Eighth Air Force carried out its largest ever operation. It involved over 2,000 bombers, which flew in support of the Allied troops fighting in the Ardennes when von Rundstedt opened up a salient or 'Bulge' in the American lines. The 388th Bomb Group put up sixty-six Fortresses on the record-breaking day when raids on airfields east of the Rhine helped prevent the *Luftwaffe* from giving more support to the German breakthrough.

On 6 February 1945 B-17G 43-37806 *Miss Fortune* was involved in a collision with B-17G 43-37894 in the 849th Bomb Squadron, 490th Bomb Group over Prickwillow, Cambridgeshire. One crew-member from each crew were killed and two civilians died and three more suffered serious injuries or burns when 43-37894 crashed on a bungalow and Lilecote Cottage.

Knettishall airfield. *(Author)*

By VE-Day, the Knettishall Group had flown 505 combat missions, dropping over 18,000 tons of bombs. Five 'Chowhound' missions were flown and 578 tons of food were delivered. Throughout the course of hostilities the 388th lost 122 Fortresses missing in action and fifty-seven to other operational causes. One of the Group's longest serving ships was *Jamaica Ginger*, which flew 157 missions.

The 388th began leaving Knettishall in June 1945 and the Group completed its return to the USA by August when the base was handed back to RAF control. The airfield was finally given up by the MoD in February 1957.

Lavenham (Cockfield) – Station 137

Lavenham airfield was completed in April 1944 by John Laing & Son Ltd, being built to the standard Class 'A' pattern with three intersecting runways, two T-2 hangars and fifty dispersed hardstandings. Named after the small picturesque town 2½ miles to the south-east, it lay between the A1141 and A134 Bury to Sudbury roads, the latter having to be slightly diverted to accommodate the western end of the main runway and dispersals. Hutted living quarters for 421 officers and 2,473 enlisted men was built to the south of the field, extending to the village of Alpheton. An English girl who lived in one the farms on the base recalled.

When the Yanks and their aircraft and vehicles arrived, it changed the area beyond recognition. All the country lanes had been widened to make room for the numerous Jeeps, command cars, large trucks and ambulances that proliferated, it seemed, overnight. By this time we had moved two miles down the road to Hopton, to a small cottage right on the road, which meant the road, was slightly wider at that point, an opportune place for two six-wheeled Studebakers or GMCs to pass. On one occasion two of these trucks tried to pass a few yards down the lane and became locked together. I can see now one of the drivers standing on the load in one truck with a crowbar, levering the sides apart, while the other drove slowly along. And the load in the truck? Bombs! They were from the main storage depot near Thetford, heading for the bomb store at Knettishall.

The 487th Bomb Group (H) arrived in early April 1944 and was to remain until the end of August 1945. This Group, which was commanded by Colonel Beirne Lay Jr, who had taken command on 28 February 1944 and the 486th Bomb Group at Sudbury (Acton), formed a two-group combat wing called the 92nd Combat Bombardment Wing. The four squadrons in the 487th Group were the 836th, 837th, 838th and 839th and these were equipped initially

Liberators in the 487th Bomb Group, taxi out at Lavenham while a formation of B-17s passes high overhead. In August the 3rd Division groups began converting from the B-24 to the Flying Fortress, and the Liberators were dispersed, chiefly among the Liberator groups of the 2nd Bomb Division. Lieutenant General Jimmy Doolittle intended to convert the 2nd Division to Fortresses as well but was prevented from doing so because there simply were not enough Fortresses to spare. (USAF)

B-17G-65-BO 43-37544 *D-Day Doll* in the 710th Bomb Squadron. *(USAF)*

with B-24H/J Liberators. The Group's distinguishing letter was a 'P in a square' on the tails. The 487th became operational during the period leading up to the Normandy landings when the Eighth was concentrating on rail and communication targets. The first mission, on 7 May, was to rail yards at Liege in Belgium. Assembly problems in the 486th Bomb Group caused the morning mission to be aborted but the afternoon mission was successful though cloud cover over the target ruled out any bombing. On this day over 1,000 US bombers were active, the main force going to Berlin.

Beirne Lay Jr, The red headed, Yale-educated, pilot and writer had penned the classic, *I Wanted Wings*, which, in 1941, had been made into a successful movie by Paramount. It was written originally to tell what happens inside a boy who 'just has to fly'. As a captain Beirne Lay Jr., had been one of Eaker's original seven senior officers who had flown

Colonel Beirne Lay Jnr. *(USAF)*

B-17G-40-BO 42-97092 *Virginia Lee II*, which was salvaged on 2 November 1944 after a crash but still made it home to the ZOI in 1945. *(USAF)*

to England with the general in 1942. When Major William Wyler, the famous Hollywood director arrived in England late in 1942 to make a documentary about 8th Air Force operations, he was given a great deal of help by General Eaker and his subordinate staff, not least Lieutenant Colonel Beirne Lay Jnr. (The movie was subsequently based around the crew of the *Memphis Belle* and the rest as they say, is history). Lay spent the early part of the war 'flying a desk' but had clamoured for action. While still a staff officer at High Wycombe he had flown the Regensburg shuttle mission on 17 August 1943 with a 100th Bomb Group crew at Thorpe Abbotts. Lay's classic, *I Saw Regensburg Destroyed*, which appeared in the 6 November 1943 issue of the Saturday Evening Post, is among the finest pieces of literature in the annals of aviation.

On the Group's fourth mission on 11 May the 92nd Wing formation was briefed to bomb the marshalling yards at Chaumont but the leading 487th Bomb Group flew into a flak area near Châteaudun. Both the lead aircraft *Peg O My Heart* and the deputy lead, *Mean Widdle Kid* and *Lazy Lady* were shot down. Four men in

B-17G-40-VE 42-97976 *A Bit O' Lace* in the 709th Bomb Squadron. *(USAF)*

the lead ship evaded capture. One of them was Colonel Beirne Lay Jr, He recalled:

> I was riding in the co-pilot's seat and witnessed the explosion of my No. 3 man's B-24, busy at the time though I was with our own battle damage. The first burst was right in front of the nose, a blinding flash and flames where a B-24 had just been. My biggest worry while Walt Duer and I were evading capture for three weeks was falling into the clutches of the Gestapo. They were accountable to nobody and I knew that they would never believe me when I told them that I, a Group Commander, did not know the date of D-Day (which we did not at that level) and that they would give me the works.

Colonel Lay returned to England and in 1946 he and Major Sy Bartlett, who as a major, had been General Carl Spaatz's aide, wrote the script for the film *Twelve O'clock High*, which has become a movie classic.

Colonel Robert Taylor III assumed command of the 487th Bomb Group after Lay was shot down and he remained in command until the end of 1944. The remainder of May was mostly taken up with missions to communications and airfield targets. Heavy ground mist on 20 May caused a number of take-off and assembly accidents, including two in the 486th and one in the 487th (B-24H 42-52743), which crashed near Long Melford. Lieutenant Everett F. Goethe and five of his crew in the 837th Bomb Squadron were killed and the Liberator crashed at Kentwell Hall. The force went to marshalling yards at Liège and Brussels but cloud prevented successful bombing, On 30 May better visibility permitted air-fields in the Münster area to be bombed. From this the 487th lost one B-24 in action and one ditched off Lowestoft on return. Eight of the crew were rescued. The *Virgin Vampire* flown by Lieutenant Bernard J. Majerus, which had been hit by flak and was coming in to land with No. 4 engine feathered and a smoking No. 3 engine, had no brakes and it crashed into Lieutenant Arlon F. Ziegler's B-24 tearing off the tail.

On D-Day, 6 June 1944, the Lavenham Group took part in the massive softening-up assault on the Normandy beaches. Of the 2,360-odd bomber sorties flown that day, the only one lost to enemy action was from the 487th. In the week following, airfields and rail targets in France were the order of the day, but by 20 June the 487th were back on the strategic offensive with an attack on industry in the Hannover area. July saw further strikes against airfields and V-weapons sites in France. On 21 July, after forty-six missions with B-24s, the Group was taken off operations for a brief spell to convert to the B-17G when the standardization of the whole of the 3rd Bomb Division to B-17s began. The Liberators

Signatures preserved in the bar in the Swan Hotel, Lavenham.
(Author)

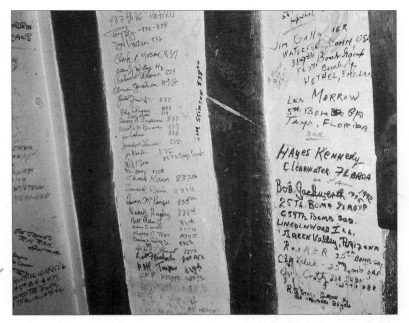

More recent signatures in the bar in the Swan Hotel, Lavenham. *(Author)*

were returned to Strategic Air Depots for re-allocation to the 2nd Bomb Division, which remained wholly equipped with the Liberator.

Back in action on 1 August, together with the Sudbury group, which had also converted to B-17s, the 92nd Combat Bombardment Wing attacked Tours airfield. Oil refineries, aircraft and tank factories in Northern and Central Germany were hit during August and included missions to Magdeburg, Mannheim, Ludwigshafen, Kiel, Bremen and Berlin, Occasional strikes on airfields and V-weapon sites were still carried out and batteries in the Brest area of France were hit on 26 August. The latter part of the month brought a spell of bad weather, which restricted operations. A major assault on German oil industry over three days 11–15 September, brought strong *Luftwaffe* opposition, resulting in the loss of ninety heavies over this period although only one of this number came from the 487th. Other targets hit by the Group during September included Düsseldorf, a tank factory at

Nuremberg, Kassel, Bremen and oil refineries at Merseburg. On the 17th the Group was among those that supported the Allied airborne landings in Holland.

By October frequent cloud cover called for increasing use of GH, H_2X and Micro H radar navigation and bombing aids. Berlin, Mainz, Cologne, Kassel and Münster were visited during this month. On 16 November a mission in support of ground troops to the east of Aachen was undertaken, but bad weather again restricted operations afterwards.

A reorganization on 21 November brought 486 and 487 Groups under control of the 4th Bomb Wing, making this the largest combat wing in the 8th AF with five groups. Heavy flak damaged a large number of bombers during the attack on the Merseburg/Leuna oil installations on 25 November. One of the 487th's Fortresses was shot down on this mission and it crashed at Framlingham on return, where one crewmember was killed. Marshalling yards, airfields and oil installations were again primary targets throughout December whenever weather permitted.

24 December 1944 was a red-letter day for the 487th Bomb Group, which led the largest Eighth Air Force mission of the war when over 2,000 bombers, escorted by nearly 1,000 fighters took off to bomb airfields east of the Rhine. Task force commander was Brigadier-General Fred Castle, commander of the 4th Bomb Wing, who led the 3rd Bomb Division on his 30th mission in *Treble Four* (44-8414) a 487th Bomb Group Fortress, with Lieutenant Robert W. Harriman's crew. All went well until 23,000ft over Belgium, about 35 miles from Liege, his right outboard engine burst into flame and the propeller had to be feathered.

Portrait of General Castle in the bar in the Swan Hotel, Lavenham. *(Author)*

Names of 487th Bomb Group Liberator aircraft painted in 1944 on a wall at Lavenham pictured in the 1970s. They include: *Sky Master*; *Spirit of 76*; *Box Car*; *Just F/O 20%*; *Paddlefoot*; *High Hopes*; *Our Baby*; *D'Nif Annie*; *Lumbering Lizzy* and *The Big Drip*. (*Author*)

The deputy lead ship took over and Castle dropped down to 20,000ft. But at this height the aircraft began vibrating badly and he was forced to take it down another 3,000ft before levelling out. The Fortress was now down to 180 mph indicated air speed and being pursued by seven Bf 109s of IV/JG 3. They attacked and wounded the tail gunner and left the radar navigator nursing bad wounds in his neck and shoulders. Castle could not carry out any evasive manoeuvres with the full bomb load still aboard and he could not salvo them for fear of hitting Allied troops on the ground. Successive attacks by the fighters put another two engines out of action and the B-17 lost altitude. To reduce airspeed the wheels of the Fortress were lowered and the crew ordered to bale out with the terse intercom message, 'This is it boys'. Castle managed to level out, long enough for six of the crew to bale out but at 12,000ft the bomber was hit in the right wing fuel-tank, which exploded, sending the B-17 into a plunging final spiral to the ground. Brigadier General Castle was posthumously awarded the Medal of Honor; the highest ranking officer in the 8th Air Force to receive the award. Harriman and Castle were buried in the American cemetery at Henri-Chattel.

December sun going down near Maycrete huts at Lavenham. The cost of a typical Ministry of Works 10-bay hut including carriage, foundations and erection, was £390. *(Author)*

January 1945 saw a resumption of the offensive against oil facilities, communications and airfields. Colonel William K. Martin who took over from Colonel Taylor at the end of the old year now led the 487th. On 6 January one of the group's Fortresses crash-landed at Alpheton shortly after take off and on the 8th another crash-landed on a farm near St. Margaret's in Kent when returning from a mission. The latter part of January and early February brought more bad weather which restricted operations but another major attack on Berlin was launched on 6 February when one more of the 487th's B-17s crashed on its home base on return. The marshalling yards at Hamm on 16 November and Nuremberg on the 20th and 21st were among the targets pounded during February while on 22nd–23rd Operation Clarion, a major assault on road and rail communications, took place followed by another visit to Berlin.

The introduction of enemy jet-fighters in 1945 caused some concern, but any large build-up was partly neutralized by attacks on their airfields. U-boat yards at Hamburg were on the mission list for March. Hannover was the target on the 14th when an 836th Bomb Squadron Fortress aborted and crashed at Carlton

Reflections in time. Lavenham control tower. *(Author)*

Colville near Lowestoft, killing two crew. (See Carlton Colville entry in Appendix 1). The following day two more crash-landed in liberated Poland. Concentrated attacks by enemy jet fighters during the Berlin mission of 18 March caused some casualties. One of the Group's Forts crash-landed in Soviet territory and a collision over Allied territory wrote off two more when returning from attacks on jet airfields. Another large-scale mission in support of Operation Varsity (the Rhine crossing) was carried out on 24 March when 1,750 heavies were dispatched to airfields in west

The former fire station beside the control tower at Lavenham. *(Author)*

Sun glints on the rain soaked concrete at Lavenham where once hundreds of American bombers flew. *(Author)*

and north-west Germany. With the end of the war in sight, enemy fighter opposition slackened off but flak still continued to claim a number of victims, four of which were from the Lavenham Group during attacks on airfields in the Brandenburg area on 10 April. Strong-points in the Bordeaux area of France were attacked on 14 and 15 April and on 17 April, targets in south-east Germany were hit. The Group's final combat mission was on 21 April when airfields at Landsberg were bombed. In all the 487th Bomb Group flew 185 missions and dropped 14,041 tons of bombs. From January 1945 they held the 3rd Division record for bombing accuracy, with strikes within 1,000ft of the MPI. Losses overall totalled forty-eight aircraft missing in action with a further thirty-seven written off to other operational causes. The Fortresses flew home during the first week of July 1945 and by the end of August the remaining personnel had left for the States.

The English girl who lived in one the farms on the base recalled:

They went shouting and singing and waving. We could hear them as they went along the road to the station, until they got farther and farther away, then everywhere became silent. The Yanks had come, and now they were gone! I shall always remember that vast contrast when they left. One moment it

Lavenham is perhaps the best preserved medieval town in Britain, a centre of the medieval wool and cloth industry where the lath-and-plaster timber-framed dwellings, all bright pink and yellow so typical of this area are numerous. Among the finest is the guildhall in the main square (top left) and the half timbered Swan Hotel (middle, right).
(Author)

was all noise, shouting, trucks starting and stopping and then dead silence, with everything deserted. I walked back home across the runway. There was no one in sight; it was just as if everyone had fallen asleep. We should never forget the 390th, the boys who had come so far from their homes in America, many of them never to return. For more than two years they lived in and were a part of our countryside and we sincerely missed them when they were gone.

The airfield was handed back to the RAF and placed on a care and maintenance basis with Transport, Maintenance and Bomber Commands each taking a share in the control, although no aircraft are known to have been deployed there. The airfield was finally sold off in 1958.

Mendlesham (Wetheringsett) – Station 156

The flying field was constructed to the standard Class 'A' specification with one 2,000-yard runway and the other two of 1,400 yards each. The perimeter track was three-and-a-half miles long and, of the fifty hardstandings, forty-eight were hoops and two of the frying-pan type. Hangars were the usual two T2s and all buildings were temporary, chiefly Nissen huts. The accommodation catered for 2,972 personnel. The first flying unit to use Mendlesham was 310 (Czechoslovakian) Squadron equipped with Spitfire IXs, which arrived in February 1944 and left in April. the base then became the home of the 34th Bomb Group, which was commanded by Colonel Ernest J. Wackwitz, until August 1945. Although activated in 1941, the group had remained Stateside to train other cadres and had only left the US in late March 1944. During their combat period, the group flew 170 missions from Mendlesham, the first sixty-two in B-24H/J Liberators and the rest with B-17G Fortresses. The changeover was made during the summer of 1944 when, in common with other groups assigned to the 93rd Combat Wing, the 3rd Division standardised on the Fortress.

B-17G-50-VE 44-8158 *Bobby Sox* which served in the 4th Bomb Squadron, 34th Bomb Group, 850th Bomb Squadron, 490th Bomb Group and the 332nd Bomb Squadron, 94th Bomb Group before being scrapped at Walnut Ridge in December 1945. *(USAF)*

On 23 May 804 B-17s and B-24s including for the first time, the 34th Bomb Group, bombed several targets including Hamburg, Saarbrücken and French airfields. During its relatively short combat history the Group lost thirty-four aircraft yet the only losses to enemy aircraft were over Mendlesham. On 7 June 1944, at dusk, as its aircraft were returning from a mission over France, Me 410 intruders of KG51 'Edelweiss' shot down four Liberators in a matter of minutes over the airfield killing at least thirteen aircrew. Wilson (42-52738) crashed into an equipment store, *Sweet Sioux* (formerly *Piccadilly Tilly*, 42-94911) fell at Joe's Road, Wetheringsett destroying three thatched cottages. *Glamor Girl* (41-29572) crashed at Nedging. *Cookie's Wailing Wall* (42-52696) crash-landed on Eye airfield, as Captain Oscar T. Hanson, who had flown his first mission on D-Day, recalled:

Several ships went down in flames. I heard a terrific explosion in the back of the ship and we were on fire. I gave the order to bale out and started climbing as we were only at 1,000ft. I climbed to 7,000ft and set the automatic pilot so I could head the ship out to sea. I expected to get hit again and everyone baled out except my engineer and myself. He noticed that the fire had gone out so he inspected the damage. I spotted a blacked-out airport in the moonlight so we decided to land. Our hydraulic system was shot so we had to crank the landing gear down mechanically and we had no brakes and no flaps. When the gear came down we could see that our wheel was so badly damaged it would collapse on landing. We made two passes at the field and them came in to land, skidding along the ground for a while and then turning sideways as the wing-tip was dragging on the ground. Our landing speed without flaps was 120mph. Due to the danger of getting strafed by the enemy, the field was not lighted and I could just barely see the runways in the moonlight. They told us afterward that one of the fighters was looking for us but he was circling the field to the right and we were circling to the left and we passed each other twice over the field! We returned to our home field and the rest of the crew who had baled out straggled in one by one. None of the crew was killed. When we went back to look at our ship the next day we counted fourteen holes from 20mm cannon. The ship was peppered with shrapnel and it was miraculous that no one

B-17G-80-VE 44-8731 *Knockout Dropper* in the 391st Bomb Squadron, in 1945. *(USAF)*

was hit. The nose gunner broke his leg when he landed. The co-pilot jumped without his leg straps fastened and came very near to falling out of his chute. The tail gunner's chute failed to open so he fed it out with his hands. The radio operator pulled four times on the wrong handle before

Cartoon that adorned a wall at Mendlesham in the 1970s. *(Steve Gotts)*

A GI throwing his money around on a wall at Mendlesham. *(Author)*

Cartoon at Mendlesham in the 1970s. *(Author)*

18th Bomb Squadron insignia now removed to Horham. *(Author)*

finding the ripcord and the bombardier landed right on our
home field and was immediately surrounded by GIs who
thought he was a German paratrooper. He said, 'Don't click
them bolts at me, Ah'm from Texas!'

(Hanson, who received the DFC, was KIA on the mission to
Merseburg on 30 November 1944).

In the course of its 170 combat missions the Group lost
thirty-four aircraft. These included, on 22 June, Lieutenant Guy
M. Gipson's B-24, *Off Limits*, which was hit by flak at Tournay-
Sur-Brie and was then attacked by Fw 190s of JG 26 but made it
back and crashed at Denge Beach near Dungeness. On 18 August
1944, three B-24s on the raid on an airfield in France, near Amiens.
On 24 August, the last mission flying Liberators, B-24J 44-40443
in the 4th Squadron crashed at Holt, Norfolk killing eight of the
crew. Only the pilot, Major Joseph O. Garrett the 4th Squadron
CO, survived. On 5 January 1945 when the severe wintry weather

Abandoned buildings at Mendlesham. *(Author)*

The 34th Bomb Group memorial by the A140 at Mendlesham. *(Author)*

over England was responsible for several fatal accidents during take-off for a mission to Frankfurt a 34th Bomb Group Fortress came to grief while attempting take-off. Mendlesham was no longer used for regular flying after the Americans left in the late

Mendlesham airfield in 2008. *(Author)*

summer of 1945 and it became a sub-site of No. 94 Maintenance Unit being used as an ammunition storage depot. It was reduced to inactive status in June 1954. After St. Ives Sand & Gravel Company had finished their work on the site, the technical area was used for warehousing. The television mast for Anglia TV was erected on the former HQ site during the 1950s.

13

Rattlesden – Station 126

Built by George Wimpey & Co. Ltd., in 1942 as a Class 'A' bomber airfield, Rattlesden had three intersecting concrete runways, perimeter track and, for USAAF use, hardstandings for fifty aircraft and two dispersed, black-painted T2 hangars. Living and messing sites were on the east side of the field. Situated 4 miles south of the A14 between Stowmarket and Bury St. Edmunds, Rattlesden (actually closer to the village of Felsham) was originally a satellite for Rougham (Bury St. Edmunds), both being assigned to the 3rd Bomb Wing which controlled most of the USAAF-occupied airfields in Suffolk. The mission of this wing was medium bombardment and Rattlesden was destined to receive B-26 Marauders when, in December 1942, the ground personnel of two squadrons (451st and 452nd) of the 322nd Bomb Group moved in. In April 1943, however, the units were moved to the main base at Bury St. Edmunds (Rougham) after a decision to establish one group per airfield, leaving Rattlesden awaiting another B-26 group.

In June, it was decided that the B-26 groups would be better placed to conduct operations from airfields further south, and an exchange of bases with the B-17-equipped 4th Bomb Wing in Essex was arranged. Rattlesden, however, remained without a combat unit until November when a new Fortress group, the 447th Bomb Group commanded by Colonel Hunter Harris Jnr, arrived. The 447th became a part of the 4th Combat Bombardment Wing,

B-17G-70-BO 43-37797 CD-U *American Beauty* in the 708th Bomb
Squadron, which came to grief at Rattlesden on 9 January 1945. The
aircraft was repaired and she finished her days at Kingman, Arizona, in
December 1945. *(via Ian McLachlan)*

the other two groups of the wing being the 94th at Rougham
and the 385th at Great Ashfield. Recognized by the big square
'K' on their tails, the B-17Gs of the 447th Bomb Group were in
four squadrons: the 708th, 709th, 710th and 711th Bombardment
Squadrons. The 447th flew their first mission from Rattlesden on
Christmas Eve 1943 when the target was 'Noball' sites in the Pas
de Calais. All the aircraft returned though several were damaged.
On 11 January 1944 the target for a large force of 8th AF bombers
was aircraft plants in the Brunswick area. As often happened,
heavy cloud built up during the outward flight and most of the
force was recalled. However, the 4th Combat Bombardment Wing,
led by Lieutenant Colonel Louis G. Thorup riding with the 94th,
was quite close to its allotted target: the Me 110 plant at Waggum
and decided to carry on to achieve some excellent bombing
results. The newly-blooded 447th placed about 75 per cent of their
bombs within 1,000ft of the MPI, although they lost three of their
number during heavy fighting in which the 8th lost a total of
sixty aircraft. During the course of hostilities the 447th flew 257
missions from Rattlesden and the 447th achieved one of the best
overall bombing accuracy records in the 3rd Division.

April 1944 proved to be an unlucky month for the 447th. On
13 April when the target was Augsburg, the Third Division lost
eighteen aircraft including three in the 447th Bomb Group, which

landed in Switzerland. One of the Group's B-17s made it home to Rattlesden only to crash in Ham Street. During bombing-up on the 21st one of the bombs exploded killing several airmen and writing off three B-17s at their dispersals. Then on 29 April the 447th incurred what was to be their biggest loss of the war. Berlin was the target with the 3rd Division leading. Due to assembly problems the force became badly strung out and presented some easy pickings for the 300-plus *Luftwaffe* fighters sent up to defend 'Big B'. The 4th Wing became separated from the main force and without fighter escort they were hit while over the Magdeburg area. In all the 447th lost eleven Fortresses, although one crew was rescued after ditching in the North Sea. In all the 8th AF lost sixty bombers. On 29 April 768 bomber crews throughout East Anglia were awakened early for the briefing for a raid on Berlin. Worst hit of all the Bomb Groups was the 447th. Sergeant Louis J. Torretta, a tail gunner, recalls:

The first attack of about eighty fighters came from 1 o'clock high. Parachutes were seen all over the sky from our ships and from the Germans also. I had given up all hope of getting back because we were the only ship left in our formation, so I reached back and grabbed my parachute only to find it too was riddled. Then one lone fighter made another attack on us and I started to shoot and I discovered one of my guns was hit by one of the enemy bullets and it wouldn't work. This fighter fired a couple of times and quit I guess he ran out of ammunition, thank God. That was the only thing that saved us because if they had had enough ammunition to make another attack we surely would have gone down. We had quite a bit of trouble with that left wing but good old Moe, our pilot, pulled us through again. Boy, what a pilot that guy is. I would fly through anything with him at the controls. Our group put twenty-one ships up in the air today and eleven of them came back. I guess that is about all. Sure am glad to be back alive from this one.

The 447th Bomb Group's eleven losses took its monthly total to twenty-one aircraft lost. Good bombing results were again recorded on 12 May when oil installations in the Leipzig area were attacked by a force of nearly 900 bombers. This also proved costly to the 4th Combat Bombardment Wing, losing eleven

B-17G-90-BO 43-38524 *Blonde Bomber II* in the 710th Bomb Squadron
finished her days at Kingman, Arizona in 1945. *(USAF)*

aircraft, seven of which were from the 447th. Along with most of
the 8th AF, the Rattlesden group undertook tactical missions in
support of the Allied armies during and after the D-Day landings.
Then it was back to the strategic campaign attacking industrial,
oil and associated targets. In September 1944 Colonel William
J. Wrigglesworth took command of the group in place of Colonel
Harris.

During the 1,000 bomber mission to Merseburg-Leuna on
2 November 2nd Lieutenant Robert E. Femoyer, a navigator in the
447th Bomb Group, was posthumously awarded the Medal of
Honor. Femoyer's B-17 was rocked by three flak bursts, which
showered the aircraft with shrapnel. Femoyer was hit in the back
and the side of his body but refused all aid despite his terrible
wounds so that he might navigate the Fortress back to Rattlesden.
He was propped up in his seat to enable him to read his charts
and the crew did what they could for him. It was not until they
reached the North Sea that Femoyer agreed to an injection of
morphia. He died shortly after the aircraft landed.

The 447th battled on during the winter of 1944–1945 to a wide
range of targets besides carrying out a number of supply drops

in the following spring. By this time the B-17Gs were sporting yellow vertical tail surfaces and two parallel green bands round the rear fuselage. Most of the Olive Drab (OD) and grey B-17s had long since been replaced by newer examples with natural metal factory finish. During one of the last missions of the war, to marshalling yards in south-east Germany on 19 April, the 447th lost their last B-17 to enemy action. Me 262 jets attacked the Fortress, flown by Lieutenant R. Glazner in the high squadron. The crew were liberated a few days later. In the course of their missions in the ETO the 447th Bomb Group flew 257 combat missions during which 17,000 tons of bombs and nearly 400 tons of supplies were dropped. Losses were ninety-seven aircraft MIA and forty-three to other causes. One of the Group's Fortresses, *Milk Wagon*, held the Group's record of 129 missions without one abort due to mechanical faults; a fine achievement by Technical Sergeant R. Orlosky and his men, who painted milk bottles on the B-17's nose in place of the more usual bomb symbols.

The 447th left for the USA late in July 1945 and the airfield was transferred to the RAF control on 10 October 1945. For a short while the base was used as a Ministry of Food buffer depot but was finally inactivated on 15 August 1946. On 1 December 1959 266 Squadron re-formed at Rattlesden with thirty-two Blood-hound SAM missiles. This unit was sited on the south side of the airfield between the peri-track and the SE–NW runway with all the associated launchers, buildings and radar. No. 266 Squadron

Rattlesden airfield in June 2006. (*Author*)

was disbanded on 30 June 1964 and by 1968 most of the airfield had been returned to farming in the hands of the Watts family. The whole airfield was sold and returned to agricultural use, the clearance work being undertaken by St. Ives Sand and Gravel Company for sale in the Ipswich area. In 1976 the Rattlesden Gliding Club, owned by Mr R. Watts, was established on the airfield using the one operational runway and the control tower became the club house.

14

Snetterton Heath – Station 138

In 1943 Michael R. Downes, a 7 year old living in Attleborough, recalls:

> My father came home one day and said, "The Yanks are coming today", so he rigged up a seat on the crossbar of his bicycle and rode me down to Snetterton Heath about 1½ miles down the road. We waited and in they came: the planes all painted khaki. Within a matter of months we had five different air bases within a radius of five to six miles around the town of Attleborough.

The airfield was constructed by Taylor-Woodrow Ltd in 1942 at a cost of £950,000. The main runway was 2,000 yards in length and the auxiliary runways of 1,400 yards each. Originally thirty-six hardstandings of the 'frying pan' type were provided as, when work started, the base was intended for RAF use. When rescheduled for the USAAF, the number was increased to fifty, all hardstandings being on the south and eastern side of the airfield as a railway line and the A11 road restricted dispersed locations. Total area of concrete laid in its construction was 530,000 square yards with storage provided for 144,000 gallons of fuel. Accommodations were built to house 443 officers and 2,529

B-17F-100-BO 42-30372 *Fertile Myrtle III* and B-17F-85-BO 42-30130
crossing the Alps after bombing Regensburg on 17 August 1943.
Brigadier General Curtis E. LeMay, who in July 1943 had been promoted
4th Wing CO led the raid in Captain Tom Kenny's B-17F-100-BO
42-30366, *Fertile Myrtle III* in the 338th Bomb Squadron in the leading 96th
Bomb Group. After the target the surviving 128 B-17s, some flying on
three engines and many trailing smoke, were attacked by a few fighters
on the way to the Alps. LeMay circled his formation over Lake Garda to
try to give the cripples a chance to rejoin them. Although the Snetterton
Heath group did not lose a single B-17 the 4th Wing lost twenty-four
aircraft, while sixty Fortresses which made it to North Africa had to be
left behind for repairs. *Fertile Myrtle III* was badly shot up over Bremen
on 16 December 1943 and crashed at Taverham near Norwich after being
abandoned by Kenney's crew. *(via Geoff Ward)*

enlisted men. Construction of an air depot, known as Eccles was
begun on the northern side of the airfield, access being across the
A11. Four T2 hangars were built on this site but a reduction in
the number of heavy bombers being sent to the UK led to this
depot becoming surplus to Eighth Air Force requirements and
construction was stopped before all facilities were completed.

In the spring of 1943 the first Eighth Air Force organisation to
arrive at Snetterton Heath was the 386th Bomb Group (M) with
B-26 Marauder aircraft but these remained for a week when their
place was taken by the 96th Bomb Group with B-17F Fortresses.

B-17G-1-BO 42-31118 *Lady Millicent II* in the 338th Bomb Squadron, which bellied in at Snetterton Heath on 8 January 1944 and was salvaged five days later. *(Joseph Minton via Larry Goldstein)*

This group had been based at Grafton Underwood before moving to Andrews Field, six miles from Earls Colne in Essex on 23 May where it was to become one of three B-17F groups in Essex and Suffolk in the new 4th Bomb Wing. On Sunday 13 June the 4th Wing went to Kiel for another raid on the U-boat yards and returned to England to land at their new bases in Suffolk. They replaced the Marauder Groups, which were moved out to bases further south so that fighter cover for them could be improved. The 'Snetterton Falcons' went on to fly 321 missions from the Norfolk base not far from 3rd Division Headquarters at Elveden Hall. On 17 August 1943 Colonel (later General) Curtis E. LeMay led the famous Regensburg shuttle mission to North Africa, flying in *Fertile Myrtle III!* flown by Captain Tom Kenny, at the head of the 96th Bomb Group formation. The 96th also led the 3rd Division on the Schweinfurt mission of 14 October 1943 when the former Falcons' CO, Colonel Archie Old, now CO, 45th Wing, flew in the lead ship. The 96th lost seven Fortresses including *Dottie J III* flown by 2nd Lieutenant Raymond F. Bye, which made a wheels-up landing in France.

B-17F 42-6099/R *Winnie C* in the 339th Bomb Squadron dropping bombs. This aircraft and 2nd Lieutenant Nathan L. Young's crew FTR on 22 March 1944. *(USAF)*

The 'Snetterton Falcons' finished the war with the second highest losses in the 8th Air Force and the highest of all the 3rd Division Groups. On 25 February 1944 when the USSTAF brought the curtain down on 'Big Week' and the 3rd Division was assigned Regensburg the 96th Bomb Group lost four B-17s. On Tuesday 11 April The 13th and 45th Combat Wings in the 3rd Bomb Division force were confronted with bad weather in the Poznan area and were forced to bomb the secondary target at Rostock. Rocket-firing Me 410s and Ju88s took advantage of a lapse in fighter cover and wreaked havoc among the leading groups. The 96th Bomb Group was worst hit, losing ten of the twenty-five bombers lost this day. Fred Huston, a bombardier in a 337th Bomb Squadron crew who arrived in England in the early spring of 1944 remembers:

My memory of some of the missions we flew are vivid in the extreme, others just names and how many hours it took to get there and back but the Merseburg–Lutzkendorf–Leuna missions still stand out, with a certain amount of terror included. It was the most screwed up of targets in all of Germany and every time we went there something happened either to cause us to miss the damned target or, I suspect, even to miss the European continent. Our first trip there I thought very little about it. It was just another place where the red string ended and the intelligence officer assured us was vital to the prosecution of the war. Of course, they said that about every target so we took it with a pinch of salt. Some of them didn't seem all that important to a bunch of 20 year olds who were more concerned with the next pass to London than we were with saving the world. I am sure that I went to Merseburg something like four or five times. Merseburg was the first time I saw coloured flak. I remember it as red, although there are those who remember it as pale blue. I still think it was red. We were told by someone, probably someone who didn't know either, that it was to

B-17Gs in the 413th Bomb Squadron, preparing to take off at Snetterton Heath. 43-37792/N was lost with Lieutenant Henry Chrismon's crew on the mission to Osnabrück on 21 November 1944. *(USAF)*

B-17Gs in the 96th Bomb Group taxi out at Snetterton Heath. On the runway, left, is 42-97775/L in the 413th Bomb Squadron, which crash-landed on 14 January 1945. Right, foreground, is 43-37794/T in the 337th Bomb Squadron, which was lost on 19 September 1944 with Lieutenant Raymond W. Bauman's crew (all PoW). Behind is 43-37687/Y in the 338th Bomb Squadron, which FTR when it landed on the Continent on 15 February 1945. *(USAF)*

call in the fighters. Since we already had more fighters than Custer had Sioux, I thought that it was gilding the lily somewhat to call in something that we already had in abundance. But to me, one fighter was plenty for the day.

On 12 May 1944 the 'Snetterton Falcons' were dismayed when it was revealed that Zwickau in Czechoslovakia was the target and the Group would send off twenty-six Fortresses. Although there had been no losses on the last three missions a ten-plane loss

Lieutenant Len Kramer's B-17G 43-38576 on fire after landing too close to another B-17 at Snetterton on 28 December 1944. *(USAF)*

B-17G-70-BO 43-37716 *5 Grand*, the 5,000th Boeing-built Fortress, which was liberally autographed by Boeing factory workers, flew seventy-eight combat missions, two food missions and two PoW missions in the 338th Bomb Squadron, 96th Bomb Group. Allocated to the 560th Bomb Squadron, 388th Bomb Group to be flown home for a War Bond drive, the plane left for the USA on 9 June 1945 and it was broken up for scrap at Kingman, Arizona in November that year. *(USAF)*

Officers and enlisted men 'sweating out the mission' at Snetterton Heath. Note the RAF liaison officer on the balcony of the control tower. *(USAF)*

The shuttle force touched down at Poltava, where, later that night, sixty *Luftwaffe* bombers destroyed forty-four of the seventy-two bombers, including Lieutenant Robert Wightman's B-17G-55-BO 42-102670 and severely damaging twenty-six more. *(via Geoff Ward)*

on 8 May at Brunswick coupled with twenty-six plane casualties in April created an unwanted legend in the 96th. On 12 May the 'Snetterton Falcons' mission to Zwickau cost the group twelve Fortresses (including two which collided over Germany). Among them were *Smokey Stover Jr.* and *The 7th Son* while *Silver Slipper*, which was originally listed as missing, made it back across the Channel to Manston with two engines feathered on the left side. One navigator who survived saw the lead ship pull up into a wing over with half its left wing shot off and then described how the fighters headed back through and started cutting them up. From then on it was just one long melee until finally there just wasn't any Snetterton Falcons to talk about. Warren Berg wrote in his diary:

> Today we lost the last of the seven crews who became operational when we did! The carnage was terrific: B-17s burning, exploding, plenty of enemy going down too. A dogfight whirls by us like tumbleweed, it all happens so swiftly one can't grasp the situation. The most heartening sight; four P-38s covering us from 30 FW. The Lightnings wouldn't chase but stayed close to us; I'd like to pin medals on these boys. Again they [Graves Registration] are cleaning out the belongings of what had been a brand new crew in our hut. This is the third time!

Snetterton Heath Memorial *(Author)*

When the 96th Bomb Group's last mission was flown on 25 April 1945 the losses in aircraft totalled 189 and fifty more Fortresses were lost on non-combat flights.

Snetterton Heath airfield fell into disuse after the war and was privately purchased in 1952 with a view to utilizing the runways and perimeter tracks as a motor racing circuit. The first motor cycle meeting was held in 1953 and the first motor race the following year. In March 1963, the airfield was acquired by Grovewood Securities Ltd., after which the present company organizing the racing, Snetterton Circuit Ltd, was formed. The original 2.71-mile-long track is now only used for the International Race of Aces as, in the early part of 1974, a new 1.917-mile short circuit was formed. This includes a long straight

Snetterton Heath airfield on Sunday 24 September 2006. *(Author)*

(on one of the old secondary runways) suitable for drag racing and the first dragster meeting was held on 29 September 1974. Today, banking and safety barriers have transformed the airfield and Snetterton is used extensively, not only for national, international as well as local club racing, but also for the testing and development of motor cycles and cars.

Snetterton Heath raceway just before the old A11 was broken up and replaced with the long awaited dual carriageway. *(Author)*

15

Sudbury (Acton) – Station 174

This airfield conformed to the standard Class 'A' heavy bomber base with three intersecting concrete runways of standard lengths with fifty hardstandings and two T2 hangars to meet the USAAF bomber requirement. The site had a slight gradient towards the north-east and was constructed on what had hitherto been farmland. Most of the temporary building accommodation for some 3,000 men was situated around the village street of

Sudbury airfield in June 2006. (*Author*)

Great Waldingfield to the east of the airfield and accessible by crossing the B1115 road from Sudbury to Lavenham. The 486th Bomb Group operated from this base between late March 1944 and August 1945, beginning combat operations on 7 May 1944 under the command of Colonel Glendon P. Overing and completing 188 missions on 21 April 1945. The first forty-six missions were flown in B-24H/J aircraft and the remainder in B-17Gs from 1 August 1944 to April 1945. Together with the 487th Group based at Lavenham, the 486th formed the 92nd Combat Bombardment Wing, which had headquarters at Sudbury. On 22 November 1944

Soon after the occupation of Linz, Austria, by US forces in May 1945, military government authorities organized the rapid repatriation from the district of Frenchmen and their families by US transport planes and Flying Fortresses, which made the journey from the Horching Flugplatz airfield at Linz to Le Bourget airfield near Paris in three hours. B-17Gs of the 486th Bomb Group can be seen. B-17G40-VE 42-98006/F is *The Old Yard Dog*, which finished her days at Kingman, Arizona, seven months later. Next in line are B-17G-50-DL 44-6477, B-17G-75-BO 43-37973 *The Worry Bird*, and B-17G-75-BO 43-37970. Some 38,000 Frenchmen and their families were thus transported by plane, 8,000 being carried in one day. Some of the French were 'voluntary' workers who were induced to work in Germany on the promise made by the Germans that their enrolment would release French prisoners of war. Others were slave workers and concentration camp victims. Many of the workers had their wives with them and several children were born in the work and concentration camps. *(OWI photo by E H. Davies)*

An 832nd Bomb Squadron, 486th Bomb Group B-24 Liberator passes over Allied shipping off the Normandy beachhead near Caen on D-Day, 6 June 1944. *(USAF)*

the 92nd CBW was disbanded and the 486th and 487th Bomb Groups were combined in a new 4th Wing (P) (later 4th CBW) with headquarters at Bury St. Edmunds. The 486th Bomb Group's main claim to fame was that the 834th Bomb Squadron lost no aircraft or personnel on the first 100 missions. In all, the Group lost thirty-three aircraft in combat and dropped 14,517 tons of bombs. On 15 October 1944 B-17G 43-38137 in the 835th Bomb Squadron crashed at Woodhall Farm, Sudbury killing all nine men in Lieutenant Clarence B. Hermann's crew and a civilian on the ground. On 31 December B-17G 43-37910 in the 832nd Bomb Squadron crashed at Little Cornard near Sudbury with no losses among Lieutenant Virgil G. F. Raddatz's crew.

After Sudbury was abandoned, the hangars were first used for government storage until the airfield was sold between 1962–64.

16

Thorpe Abbotts – Station 139

O f all the bombardment groups in the 8th Air Force perhaps the best known is the 100th Bomb Group. Often referred to as the 'Bloody Hundredth', in the less than two years the Group was in action in Europe, it lost 229 Fortresses (177 MIA and 52 to 'other operational losses'). This is the third highest total among 8th Air Force units: More precisely, the 100th had the highest loss rate among its sister groups for the 22 months it was operational. When it left England in 1945 the 'Bloody

B-17F-110-BO 42-30604 *Badger's Beauty V* in the 350th Bomb Squadron, which was lost on 4 October 1943 with Captain Harold B. Helstrom's crew. *(TAMM)*

Hundredth' had become perhaps the most famous, albeit, most jinxed bomb group in the Eighth Air Force. On 17 August 1943 nine B-17s were lost on the shuttle mission to the Messerschmitt factory at Regensburg. It was on this mission that the legend

Captain Thomas H. Murphy (centre kneeling), his crew and ground crew in the 351st Bomb Squadron in front of B-17F-30-VE 42-5864 *Piccadilly Lily* which Murphy and Beirne Lay Jr flew on the 17 August 1943 mission to Regensburg. Two missions short of his twenty-fifth and final sortie Murphy volunteered to fly the 8 October 1943 mission to Münster. Thomas, four of his crew and Captain Alvin L. Barker, 351st Bomb Squadron Operations Officer, who took 2nd Lieutenant Marshall F. Lee's seat with the co-pilot occupying the ball turret, were KIA. Five crew survived and were taken prisoner. Back Row L-R: Six ground crew followed by Albert C. Davis, waist gunner and Staff Sergeant John J. Ehlen, top-turret gunner (PoW). Front Row L-R: Staff Sergeant Aaron A. David, tail gunner (KIA); Staff Sergeant Gerald O. Robinson, gunner (PoW); 2nd Lieutenant Marshall F. Lee (KIA); Thomas Murphy (KIA 8.10.43); 1st Lieutenant Charles C. Sarabun, navigator (PoW); 1st Lieutenant Floyd C. Peterson, bombardier (PoW) and Emmett H. Evans, radio operator. Davis and Evans had finished their tour and were replaced on the Bremen mission by Staff Sergeant Elder D. Dickerson and Technical Sergeant Derrell C. Piel respectively, both of whom were KIA. *(TAMM)*

of the Bloody Hundredth was founded. Enemy fighters attacked Captain Robert Knox, pilot of *Picklepuss*, as he neared the target. Crews reported seeing Knox lower his undercarriage as a sign of surrender and the German fighters held their fire. Then as the 109s flew alongside, the gunners aboard the B-17 opened fire. Enraged, the *Luftwaffe* pilots attacked and shot down the Fortress, which crashed with the loss of six of the crew. It was said that thereafter the 100th was a marked group and were singled out for special attention. In reality the high losses were caused mostly by poor formation flying but the 100th's bad reputation was assured. Griswold Smith, a pilot in the 100th, adds:

> On one mission a lot of ships didn't find their own groups and tacked on to anyone they could for protection. Everybody was yelling over VHF trying to locate their own group. I heard one pilot tell his group that he couldn't locate them so he was going on in with another group. His commander called back and asked which group he was with. He replied that he didn't know but that they had black rudders and a 'D' on the tail. Someone said, "Oh, that's the 'Bloody Hundredth'". Then I saw a red tailed ship leave the squadron in front of me. Needless to say, this didn't make me feel any better.

All of this was in the future when in 1942 construction of an airfield at Thorpe Abbotts in south Norfolk 5 miles east of Diss and about one mile north of the A143 Diss–Great Yarmouth

The wrecked mid-upper turret of B-17F-120-BO 42-30796 *Sunny II* flown by John Griffin in the 351st Bomb Squadron, on the Bremen raid on 8 October 1943. An exploding 20mm shell blew away the top of the upper turret hurling Sergeant Harjo into the gangway leading into the bombardier's compartment. On landing the crew found bullet holes in all four propellers and one slug was still lodged in the right arm of the tail gunner. *(TAMM)*

On 27 December 1943 three B-17s pile up landing on the short runway at Thorpe Abbotts. *King Bee*, *Flyin Jenny* and a third Fortress were wrecked but amazingly there were no casualties. *(USAF)*

road was begun by John Laing & Sons as the main contractors. Intended as a satellite to Horham, both airfields were for RAF use but the rapid build-up of the US 8th Air Force resulted in them being handed over to the Americans. Construction work was barely finished when the 100th Bomb Group, commanded by Colonel Harold Q. Huglin, arrived on 9 June 1943 to join the 4th Bomb Wing. The 100th should have become operational on 22 June when a formation of twenty-one B-17s was to fly a diversion for 182 heavies bombing Hüls but they were delayed because of ground mists and other problems and played no major part in the proceedings. Three days later the 100th flew its first combat mission when 275 B-17s were dispatched to bomb targets in north-west Germany. The 100th was assigned Bremen. Assembly for this, their inaugural mission was poor and three B-17s were forced to abort early. There was strong fighter opposition in the target area and three of the group's B-17s 'simply disappeared'. There was only one survivor from *Angel's Tit*; all ten aboard 42-29986 were KIA and only four survived from 42-30038.

On 1 July Colonel Huglin was relieved of command 'due to stomach ulcers' and replaced by Colonel Neil 'Chick' Harding, a West Point graduate and a famed football coach for the Army. During July the 100th took part in missions to U-boat pens in France, and during 'Blitz Week' beginning 23 July. German factories and shipbuilding yards and targets in Norway were hit. On 28 July attacks on Kassel and Oschersleben cost the 8th twenty-two bombers but none came from the 100th. On 29 July eighty-one 4th Bomb Wing Fortresses attacked the Heinkel aircraft factory at Warnemünde and again the Century Bombers came through without loss. On 30 July 186 B-17s went to Kassel and the fourteen B-17s of the 100th bombed amid heavy flak. One B-17 was hit over Antwerp and came home alone on three engines, while five aircraft returned battle damaged.

B-17F-55-DL 42-3413 *Hard Luck!* in the 350th Bomb Squadron with Captain Loren Van Steenis (*The Flying Dutchman*) and his crew. *Hard Luck* flew missions for a year and a day, being lost on its sixty-second mission, on 14 August 1944 when 2nd Lieutenant Donald E. Cielewich's crew baled out and all nine men were taken prisoner. (*via Michael P. Faley*)

B-17F-55-DL 42-3413 *Hard Luck!* in the 350th Bomb Squadron
in formation. Above and behind the NMF ship is 42-31991 *Miss-Chief.*
(TAMM)

Early August 1943 saw unescorted raids on targets in the Ruhr,
France and the Low Countries as part of the Starkey deception
plan to make the Germans believe that an invasion of the French
coast was imminent. Then on 17 August the anniversary mission
of the 8th AF, the 1st and 4th Bomb Wings were assigned the
aircraft plants at Schweinfurt and Regensburg respectively. To
minimise attacks from enemy fighters the 4th Bomb Wing, led by
Colonel Curtis E. Le May, would fly on to North Africa after the
target. The 100th put up twenty-one B-17s led by Major Kidd and
Lieutenant Colonel Beirne Lay from 8th AF HQ flew as an observer
in *Piccadilly Lily* piloted by Lieutenant Thomas Murphy. Four
P-47 groups were scheduled to escort the Regensburg force but
only one group rendezvoused with the bombers as scheduled.
The long, straggling formation stretched for 15 miles and Fortresses
in the rear of the formation were left without protection at all and
in the 1½ hours preceding the bomb run, seventeen Fortresses
were shot down. Nine were from the 100th. One of the first to go

down was *Alice From Dallas* flown by Roy Clator. His two wing-men, Thomas Hummel's B-17 on the left wing and Lieutenant Ronald W. Braley's *Tweedle O' Twill* on his right went down shortly after. *High Life*, piloted by Lieutenant Donald Oakes, managed to make Switzerland. *The WAAC Hunter* flown by Henry Shotland went down in flames and was followed by *Escape Kit*, piloted by Curtis Biddick. *Flak Happy*, flown by Ronald Hollenbeck crashed into a hillside at Ghedi south of Brescia. *Oh Nausea* flown by Lieutenant Glen S. Van Noy, which had such a bad mechanical record it is believed never to have completed a sortie or·drop a bomb in anger, went down in the Mediterranean. *Picklepuss* and Robert Knox's crew never made it to Africa either but Robert Wolf's *Wolf Pack*, Major Veal's *Torchy 2nd* and *Phartzac*, flown by Captain Norman Scott with Major Gale Cleven aboard, though badly damaged all made it.

Piccadilly Lily made it to Africa and Lay's classic account of the raid called *I Saw Regensburg Destroyed*, appeared in the 6 November 1943 issue of the *Saturday Evening Post*. In 1946 when Beirne Lay co-wrote a book and screenplay with Sy Bartlett about the air war called *Twelve O' Clock High* the central character, General Frank Savage (played by Gregory Peck) flew the *Piccadilly Lily*.

Altogether, the 4th Bomb Wing lost twenty-four bombers, with the 100th's nine losses the highest loss of all. A further sixty Fortresses had to be left in Africa pending repairs. The almost

non-existent maintenance facilities in North Africa ruled out any further shuttle missions.

The heavies were stood down on 18 August. The stand down was brief, for on 19 August forty-five Fortresses of the 4th Bomb Wing were sent to bomb the airfield at Woensdrecht. The Schweinfurt losses were still having a huge

Lieutenant Robert 'Bob' Hughes, pilot of *Nine Little Yanks and A Jerk* in the 351st Bomb Squadron. *(Hughes)*

effect on the B-17 groups and for three days no Fortress missions were flown. Then, on 24 August, the 4th Bomb Wing put up forty-two B-17s for a raid on airfields. The Fortresses were out again on 27 August, when 224 B-17s were sent out on the first of the raids

B-17F-40-DL 42-3271 *Nine Little Yanks and A Jerk* in the 351st Bomb Squadron, which was originally named by Lieutenant Robert 'Bob' Hughes' crew. (Bob Hughes is standing, 2nd from right). They had picked up a brand new B-17 at Grand Island, Nebraska in June 1943 and had named that aircraft *Nine Little Yanks and A Jerk* but on arrival in England the plane was taken away for theatre modifications and the crew never saw it again. At Thorpe Abbotts they were given 42-3271, which flew its first combat mission on 17 July 1943 to Hamburg and a month later Hughes' crew named the plane *Nine Little Yanks and A Jerk*. Ground crew personnel painted the name and the shapely nude pin-up perched on a bomb was added by Frank Stevens. Bob Hughes flew *Nine Little Yanks and A Jerk* for the last time on 24 January 1944 when poor weather on the mission forced them to bring their bombs home. *Nine Little Yanks and A Jerk*, which had completed twenty-eight missions, was salvaged on 7 March after another crew took the B-17 on a practice flight but on their return to Thorpe Abbotts the left main landing gear collapsed and the Fortress suffered severe rippling of the skin which indicated irreparable twisting of the airframe. *(TAMM)*

B-17G-35-BO 42-31981 in the 350th Bomb Squadron, which crashed at
Thorpe Abbotts on 27 April 1944 when the Group flew a double mission
for the first time in the war with a raid on a 'Noball' site in France in the
morning and an airfield at Thionville in the afternoon. *(TAMM)*

against V-weapon sites, when 187 B-17s got their bombs away on
Watten. The heavies were escorted by 173 Thunderbolts; Four
B-17s were lost. Shallow penetration raids remained the order of
the day for the B-17 groups throughout September, as VIIIth BC
was not yet strong enough to mount raids deep into the *Reich*. On
2 September airfields in north-western France were bombed.

B-17F-85-BO 42-30088 *Squawkin Hawk*, the first B-17 in the Hundredth to
complete fifty missions which after being suitably adorned, was flown
back to the States on 16 May 1944 to take part in a War Bond tour.
(TAMM)

The crew of *Hang The Expense*. L-R, front: Frank Valesh; Maurice Zetlen; John Booth and John 'Dick' Johnson. Back Row. Sergeants John Mytko; Roy Urick; Louis Black; Paul Carbone; Herschel Broyles and Ernest Jordan. Legend has it that Valesh, who had a favourite saying: 'Hang the expense, give the canary another seed!' was supposed to have 'lost' five B-17s before he completed his tour on 24 July 1944 but this is not quite true and they were not all called *Hang The Expense*. *(TAMM)*

During the morning of 3 September the heavies pounded Romilly-sur-Seine and other targets in France. On 13 September VIIIth BC was officially divided into three bombardment divisions and the six B-17 groups in the 4th Bomb Wing became the 3rd Bomb Division under Major General Curtis E. LeMay. The 95th, 100th and 390th Bomb Groups (BGs) now formed the 13th Combat Bombardment Wing.

On 15 September 140 bombers attacked the Renault works and a ball-bearing plant at Paris, while a comparable force attacked airfields at Chartres and Romilly-sur-Seine. Next day the long-range B-17s of the 3rd Bomb Division flew a 920-mile, 11-hour round trip to Bordeaux to bomb an aircraft plant, their return was made in darkness. Before this mission crews, had, however, practised taking off in squadrons and assembling as a group at night. Just off the south-west coast of England the B-17 encountered heavy rainsqualls and these, plus the impending darkness, dispersed the formation. The storm front knocked radio altimeters about 1,000ft out of calibration, and many pilots got into difficulties. Three B-17s ditched in the North Sea and two others crashed,

Lieutenant John Keys flew B-17G-25-BO 42-31723/R *Sparky* in the 349th Bomb Squadron on 19 May 1944 after a 20mm shell fired by Fw 190s over Denmark on the return from Berlin had blown a large section of the tail fin away. *Sparky* was repaired and put back into service, flying again on 2 June when the B-17s bombed Boulogne. *Sparky* had been named by Clement Cowan's crew in honour of the radio operator 'Sparky' Meyers, who was KIA on 18 March 1944 when he was hit in the back by 20mm shells as he stood on an ammunition box to reach the radio room gun during an attack by fighters. 'Sparky' was buried three days later at Madingley Cemetery, Cambridge. On 29 July 1944 *Sparky* was hit by flak on the mission to the Leuna oil plant at Merseburg and was finished off by fighters. The only survivor in Jackson Phelps' crew was the tail gunner although it was thought that several other crewmembers had baled out only to be murdered by German civilians. (*TAMM*)

B-17G-10-DL 42-37800 *Piccadilly Lilly II* in the 351St Bomb Squadron, which was salvaged on 27 June 1944. *(TAMM)*

killing all ten crew in one Fortress and one crewmember in the other. In all, the 8th lost thirteen bombers on the day's raids.

On the morning of 24 September crews were alerted for a mission to Stuttgart again, but adverse weather forced its cancellation. Instead, a practice mission was flown by the 3rd Bomb Division to test new PFF (Pathfinder Force) equipment and techniques. Bomb loads were hastily changed and machine-guns reinstalled. The B-17s completed assembly without incident but over the North Sea they were bounced by about fifteen German fighters. *Damifino II* came in for some particularly heavy attacks by fighters using the sun to excellent advantage. They raked the fuselage, and a 20mm shell started a fire in the oil tank behind the No. 3 engine. Lieutenant John Gossage, pilot, held the aircraft steady while all the crew baled out. Theodore I. Don, bombardier, baled out at 1,000ft and hit the sea almost at the instant his chute deployed. He was later rescued by a flotilla of MTBs en route to the Dutch coast, but the co-pilot and the navigator were dead when they were

On 28 July 1944 B-17G-45-BO 42-97393 *Pride of the Century* in the 349th Bomb Squadron and B-15G-55-BO 42-102598 *Super Rabbit* (pictured) in the 351st Bomb Squadron, which suffered an undercarriage failure on landing, were wrecked in runway crashes at Thorpe Abbotts. *(TAMM)*

picked up. The two waist gunners and the ball turret gunner were never found. The bomber hit the sea nose down and quickly began to sink. Gossage was trapped, but managed to pull himself free and float safely to the surface.

On 8 October more than 350 bombers attacked Bremen, the 1st and 4th Bomb Wings approaching the target from two different directions in an attempt to fool the German controllers. Airborne Carpet radar jammers aboard some of the B-17s were also used for the first time. It seemed that everything was going according to plan but the German defences had already calculated the height and speed of the previous wing, and had no need to alter those calculations as the 100th sailed over the target at much the same height and speed. The lead aircraft, *Just a Snappin* flown by Captain Everett E. Blakely and Major John B. Kidd, the command pilot, was hit repeatedly and lost 3,000ft before Blakely and Kidd regained control. It made it to England and crashed at Ludham. Seven 100th Bomb Group B-17s FTR. An Fw 190A-6 flown by *Leutnant* Hans Ehlers, a 29 year old fighter pilot in 2./JG1, collided with 42-3386 *Marie Helena*, piloted by 2nd Lieutenant Raymond J. Gormley, in the low squadron. Everett Blakely saw the collision and was left with a 'very sobering feeling in the pit of the stomach'. All ten men aboard, including Gormley were KIA.

B-17F-45-VE 42-6087 *Royal Flush* in the 418th Bomb Squadron was flying
its 75th mission when it was hit by flak between the No. 3 engine and the
fuselage, causing the aircraft to spiral down and crash within sight of
Villacoublay airfield, France on 11 August 1944. Four of Lieutenant
Alfred Aske's nine-man crew; who were all on their fifth mission, were
killed including one who is believed to have been machine-gunned by
the Germans. Three of the crew were taken prisoner while Charles
Nekvasil, radio operator and Charles Barber, co-pilot, managed to escape
and return to England. *(via Chuck Nekvasil)*

Ehlers survived the mid-air collision and baled out with various
facial injuries and a double fracture of the right thighbone.
Following the collision Lieutenant Frank H. Meadows' *Phartzac*
was torn apart from what appears to have been an explosion in
the bomb bay area. 2nd Lieutenant Arthur H. Becktoft's *War
Eagle* was observed leaving the formation under control with its
No. 3 engine on fire. It crashed with the loss of one KIA and nine
PoW. The four surviving B-17s owed their survival to the 390th
Bomb Group leader, Major Robert O. Good, who encouraged
them to move in tightly behind his twenty B-17s after the target.
The 8th lost twenty-six bombers, fourteen of them from the 3rd
Bomb Division.

B-17G-20-DL 43-37935 in the 418th Bomb Squadron, which suffered a taxi accident at Thorpe Abbotts on 1 September 1944 and was salvaged two days later. *(TAMM)*

On 9 October 378 heavies were dispatched to targets in East Prussia and Poland on its longest mission to date. Some 115 aircraft were dispatched to the Arado aircraft component plant at Anklam near Peenemünde as a diversion for 263 4th Bomb Wing bombers attacking the Polish port of Gydnia and the Focke-Wulf plant at Marienburg. The Gydnia force had continued on its 1,500-mile round trip to the docks' area. Anti-aircraft defences had been thought unnecessary so far from England, and their absence meant that the force could bomb from between 11,000 and 13,000ft with great accuracy and the Marienburg plant was destroyed. Twenty-eight bombers FTR.

At Thorpe Abbotts Major John 'Bucky' Egan, CO, 418th Bomb Squadron received permission from Colonel 'Chick' Harding to lead the group to Münster on 10 October. He was determined to avenge the loss of his close friend, Major Gale 'Bucky' Cleven, who had failed to return from Bremen on 8 October. Egan wrote,

The briefing was the same as usual, until the S-2, my good friend Miner Shaw, flashed the photo picture of the old walled city of Münster. Shaw's voice droned on that we were going to sock a residential district. At this point I found myself on my feet cheering. Others who had lost close friends in the past few raids joined in the cheering. It was a dream mission to avenge the death of a buddy. The mission had not been set up for me to kill the hated Hun but as a last resort to stop rail transportation in the Ruhr Valley. Practically all of the rail workers in the valley were being billeted in Münster. It was decided that a good big bomber raid could really mess up the very efficient German rail system by messing up its personnel. Crews were told, 'Your MPI will be Münster Cathedral . . .'.

At 13.48 hours Colonel John K. Gerhart, CO, 95th Bomb Group, took off from Horham to lead the 13th Wing to Münster. Following closely behind came the 390th and the 100th led by Egan and John Brady in *Mlle. Zig Zag*. By the time the 3rd Bomb Division crossed the Dutch coast twenty-seven aircraft had aborted with mechanical problems. The 100th had lost seven of its original twenty-one aircraft, including one, which had failed to take off from Thorpe Abbotts. Meanwhile, a diversionary force of B-24s was forced to abort, and as this formation turned for home the German controllers redirected their fighters towards the 3rd Bomb Division. At 1453 hours, just nine minutes from the target, the fighter attacks began. First to attack were the single-engine fighters, which paused only when the flak opened up at the approach to the target. They resumed their attacks again after the *Zerstören* waded in with rocket attacks to add to the carnage. Worst hit was the unlucky 13th Combat Bombardment Wing. The 100th were the low section and the *Luftwaffe* took just seven minutes to tear the 'Bloody Hundredth' formation apart.

Over the Ruhr the notorious flak batteries opened up. Several aircraft were hit, including *Mlle. Zig Zag*. Egan wrote:

Brady made the sign of the cross just as the first burst of flak went off . . . one of those close ones with red centres. [Flak killed one of Egan's waist gunners and wounded the ball turret gunner]. Just as we approached the IP, I called out to the group that our high cover was leaving, watched them go, looked straight ahead and said, "Jesus Christ! Pursuits at 12 o'clock. Looks like they're on to us!"

A rocket hit *Mlle. Zig Zag* in her belly and she dived for the ground, quickly followed by the two wingmen. Brady fought the controls while Egan organised the bale out. The engineer checked the rear of the ship while the bombardier made certain that those in the nose had gone. Egan and Brady scrambled to the bomb bay

B-17G-50-VE 44-8183 LD-Q in the 418th Bomb Squadron, at its snowy revetment in early November 1944. A terrific snowstorm blanketed East Anglia on 9 November as the Group narrowly avoided colliding with other groups returning from the mission to support ground forces near Metz. 44-8183 suffered battle damage on the mission to Hamm on 26 November and force landed at St. Trond, Belgium. It was repaired and returned to Thorpe Abbotts before flying home to the ZOI for scrapping at Walnut Ridge. (TAMM)

B-17G-100-BO 43-38963/E in the 351st Bomb Squadron, in early November 1944. This Fortress and Lieutenant Lawrence L. Bazin's crew FTR on 10 April 1945 when they crash landed at Jemmeritz. One man evaded, five were KIA and four were taken prisoner. (TAMM)

B-17G-75-BO 43-38011 *The Reluctant Dragon* in the 349th Bomb Squadron, which was named after the Walt Disney movie of 1941. *The Reluctant Dragon* suffered such severe battle damage on the mission to Merseburg on 30 November 1944 that it was deemed uneconomical to repair.
(TAMM)

and both stood on the catwalk doing an 'after you, no after you' act for a few precious seconds. Suddenly, .30 calibre shells ripped through the fuselage six inches apart in a neat row about 6 inches below their feet and both men jumped without further ceremony! Egan finally landed in a wood and after evading immediate capture, was ultimately caught and sent to PoW camp where he was reunited with his buddy 'Bucky' Cleven (who escaped to England in 1945).

The 100th reeled under the incessant attacks and eleven aircraft were shot down before the target. Only Captain Keith Harris in the 390th Bomb Group, who was flying in *Stork Club* in the 100th formation, Lieutenant Robert Rosenthal, and Lieutenant John Justice's *Pasadena Nena*, reached the target. (Justice was shot down on the homeward leg.) *Royal Flush*, which was flown by Robert Rosenthal because *Rosie's Riveters*, his usual aircraft, was still under repair following Rosie's debut on the disastrous mission to Bremen, lost two engines over Münster and a rocket shell tore through the right wing, leaving a large hole. Despite

B-17G-90-BO 43-38514 *E-Z Goin* in the 349th Bomb Squadron, which was hit by a *Rammjäger* on 7 April 1945. Joe Martin got the badly damaged Fortress back to Thorpe Abbotts where the damage was soon repaired by fitting a new rear half to the fuselage. *(TAMM)*

B-17G-35-BO 42-31991 *Miss-Chief* in the 350th Bomb Squadron, which was involved in a taxi incident with B-17G-95-BO 43-38681 in the 349th Bomb Squadron on 14 May 1945. Both aircraft were salvaged. *(TAMM)*

this, Rosenthal completed the bomb run and instigated a series of violent manoeuvres to throw the aim of the flak guns. It was a great relief when the white vapour trails of the Thunderbolt escort were seen directly ahead. There were few B-17s for the 'little friends' to protect. It had been a black day for the 13th Combat Bombardment Wing, which had lost twenty-five of the twenty-nine B-17s lost by the 3rd Bomb Division. Worst of all; the 100th had lost twelve bombers which brought its total losses to nineteen in three days. New crews replaced those lost on the mission and were subjected to the usual 'flakking process'. A new crew, which arrived at Thorpe Abbotts, heard shouts of 'fresh meat' and 'meat on the table', coming from the combat barracks.

One of the replacements was Crew 13 and Technical Sergeant Earl Benham was the radio operator. On arrival, they were told, 'You fellers are Crew 13. This is the 13th Wing. You're assigned to airplane No. 13. Oh yes, your airplane is named *Hard Luck*! (B-17F 42-3413 *Hard Luck* was a lucky ship despite its name derived from the date of its arrival with the Group, Friday 13 August 1943, and the serial number). Seven of Crew 13 finished their tour. The navigator was KIA after Benham, who flew twenty-eight combat missions, went home to the USA in 1945. The bombardier and one of the waist gunners were grounded with wounds. *Hard Luck* held what must have been a record in the 8th AF, its first fifty missions being flown with original engines. Crew chief Master Sergeant 'Zip' Myers was extremely proud of

Lieutenant Carl Thorkelson landed B-17G-85-VE 44-8834/G at Chartres airfield in France with a group of French workers as passengers during 100th Bomb Group repatriation missions in June 1945. (*TAMM*)

'his ship' and refused to allow inexperienced pilots to fly it, 'that is if it could be avoided!' (*Hard Luck* flew missions for a year and a day, being lost on its 63rd mission, on 14 August 1944).

Still licking its wounds after the severe maulings of 8 and 10 October, the 'Bloody Hundredth' was nevertheless expected to participate in Mission No. 115, to Schweinfurt, which went ahead on 14 October. Of 320 B-17s and B-24s dispatched to Schweinfurt, only 229 were effective. The 3rd Bomb Division lost fifteen Fortresses yet the 100th suffered no loss.

The losses and a spell of bad weather restricted the bombers to just two more missions in October. On base chaplains were always in attendance especially when losses mounted, but sometimes even their enthusiasm got the better of them, as Bill Carleton, 351st Bomb Squadron Engineering Officer, relates:

To further acquaint him with flying, one of our Chaplains requested permission to go along on one of the test flights. This was granted but, unfortunately, engine trouble developed. Emergency procedure was immediately utilised which included the opening of the bomb bay doors for emergency bale out. The Chaplain, who was in the cockpit, asked how his parachute worked. He was told to put his hand on the red handle, jump, count three and pull the handle. With that, the crew went back to the emergency at hand. Suddenly, the co-pilot said, "My God, there's a 'chute!" A quick check indicated that, sure enough, they were short one man. The

Chaplain had gone. The crew radioed the tower for a jeep to pick up the errant cleric and returned to base to report on the Chaplain lost on a flight over England.

On 3 November 566 B-17s and B-24s were dispatched to Wilhelmshaven and twenty-three B-17s in the 100th bombed without loss. Two days later 323 B-17s bombed Gelsenkirchen. The raid cost the 100th one B-17 and seven damaged, including *Mismalovin*, flown by Stewart McClain, which was so riddled with holes that it looked like a 'mechanised snood'. (On 25 February *Mismalovin* and Lieutenant Stewart A. McClain's crew crashed into the Channel; eight KIA two PoW). A radio operator was killed aboard *Nine Little Yanks and A Jerk* when he was struck near his collarbone by a flak fragment just above his protective flak vest. On 11 November the bombers set out for Münster but bad weather and a failure of PFF aircraft caused the 95th, 96th, 100th and 388th Bomb Groups to turn back before the enemy

Mass formation of 100th Bomb Group B-17Gs with newly applied 'Buzz Numbers' on the undersides of their left wings. Nearest two aircraft are LDY and 44-8156 LDU in the 418th Bomb Squadron. *(TAMM)*

Ground crew working on the port-inner engine of B-17G-55-BO 42-102611 *Boss Lady* in the 350th Bomb Squadron, at Thorpe Abbotts.
(TAMM)

coast. On 13 November PFF again failed, on the mission to Bremen and the eighteen B-17s in the 100th formation salvoed their bombs in the North Sea. On 16 November the 100th attacked a generating plant at Vermark in the Rjukan Valley in Norway and on 26 November, 633 heavies, the largest formation so far assembled, bombed targets as far apart as Bremen and Paris. Twenty-nine B-17s including one from the 100th, whose crew was on their first mission, were lost.

One of the most colourful pilots at Thorpe Abbotts was Frank Valesh. On 26 November 1943 Valesh, along with two friends, pilot Russell 'Pinky' Flack and navigator Andrew Campion, was given permission to slow time (test) a new engine on *Hang The Expense*. Two American Red Cross girls were also smuggled aboard. Unfortunately for Valesh the tail wheel was locked. He applied the brakes, careered off the runway hitting a tent on the way, heading for farmer Billy Draper's meadow and Lodge Farm.

B-17G-30-VE 42-97829 *Regal Eagle* in the 350th Bomb Squadron, which was one of eight Group losses on the mission to the Leuna oil plant on 29 July 1944. All nine of Lieutenant Gerald H. Steussy's crew survived and they were taken prisoner. *(TAMM)*

Hang The Expense hit a tree and crashed in the farmyard. Ken Everett, now a valued member of the Tower Museum recalls:

About a minute before Frank's sudden arrival, Billy had been working where *Hang The Expense* came to a halt and was walking to the other end of the farmyard to collect a piece of chain. If that piece of chain had been available where he was working he without doubt would have been under the wreckage of the building.

Fortunately, no one suffered serious injury but after getting out of hospital Valesh, Flack and Campion were court martialled on 20 January 1944. They were charged with the 'unauthorised flying of civilians' and fined $100 each. Four days later *Hang The Expense II* lost most of its tail to flak over Ostend on the aborted mission to Frankfurt. The tail gunner, Roy Urick, was blown out but survived and was taken prisoner. Valesh and his co-pilot, John Booth, miraculously flew the badly damaged B-17 to England and put down safely at Eastchurch. On 19 May 1944 Valesh ran off the runway, in a Pathfinder, again named *Hang The Expense*,

B-17G-55-BO 42-102649 *Lady Geraldine* arrived at Thorpe Abbotts in early
April 1944 and survived combat before being transferred to the 482nd
Bomb Group on 25 May 1945 in exchange for a newer radar ship. *Lady
Geraldine* was scrapped at Kingman, Arizona in December 1945. *Lady
Geraldine*'s nose art shows three pairs of feet, two of which are male and
the middle set, female. Originally the middle set of feet were down-
turned but these were changed on the orders of the top brass! After flying
seventy-five missions *Lady Geraldine*, which was transferred to the 482nd
Bomb Group in exchange for a newer PFF ship, finished her days at
Kingman, Arizona in 1945. *(USAF)*

belonging to the 96th Bomb Group. Valesh completed his tour on
24 July 1944, having written off two more aircraft called *Hang The
Expense*.

Meanwhile, on 30 December 1943 the 3rd Bomb Division
attacked the IG Farbenindustrie chemical works at Ludwigshafen.
The 100th lost two B-17s by the time it reached the English
Channel after the target. The first, *Laden Maiden*, piloted by
Lieutenant Marvin Leininger and Albert Witmyer, was reported
to fall behind and go down in flames after being followed by three
Fw 190s. Only the navigator, Leonard McChesney, and bombardier,
Charles Compton, survived. Both evaded capture and returned to
England by 17 April 1944. All ten men aboard *Heaven Can Wait*
baled out after an enemy fighter attack damaged the radio room
with its 20 mm cannon, starting a fire, probably in the oxygen
tanks. Both pilot Francis Smith and the co-pilot, James Law,
were taken prisoner. The rest of the crew who were on their 5th

B-17G-35-DL 42-107233 *Humpty Dumpty* was assigned to the 351st Bomb Squadron, in May 1944. Sergeant Frank 'Steve' Stevens, whose workshop was close to hardstand No. 6 where ground crew chief Master Sergeant Ray Christopher maintained the B-17, painted superb artwork based on *Forced Landing*, one of the famous Gil Elvgren creations in the Brown & Bigelow calendar. On New Year's Eve 1944 on the mission to Hamburg *Humpty Dumpty* was among the twelve B-17s in the 100th Bomb Group that FTR. All nine of Lieutenant Wallace Wilson's crew, on their 13th mission, survived, though Wilson suffered a badly injured leg and Herman Eckmeyer, the toggelier (the man who toggled or tumbled the bombs out of the bomb bay when the signal was received from the lead bombardier in the lead ship) hit the left side of the ship, injuring his ankle. *Humpty Dumpty* had flown more than sixty-seven missions.
(USAF)

mission, successfully evaded, spending some comfortable time in Paris. Lieutenant Dean Radtke, barely made it back after being hit by sustained flak in the target area and was then attacked by two Fw 190s south-west of Abbeville. In all, six B-17s returned with battle damage.

On 5 January 1944 a mid-air collision was responsible for a Fortress from another group falling on the Thorpe Abbotts' bomb dump. The aircraft's two 2,000lb bombs exploded and a thick column of smoke mushroomed skywards. The concussion set off the other bombs in the bomb dump, then machine gun fire was heard. The tannoys crackled out, "Every man for himself. Get

A Frosty day at Thorpe Abbotts. *(TAMM)*

off the base!'' George, the landlord of the Horseshoes pub at Billingford, had never had it so good!

The 100th Bomb Group took part in Operation Argument and 'Big Week', 20–25 February, and the first USAAF attack on 'Big-B': Berlin. Pilot Griswold Smith recalls:

> At briefing, when they were pulling the curtain back from the map on which our route to the target was always marked with a red ribbon, it looked as if the ribbon was never going to stop. This was always a dramatic moment because no one ever knew where the mission was going until the lights were turned off and the curtain withdrawn. When the curtain was half-way drawn you could hear 'Berlin' whispered all over the room. My heart quickened a little.

The 3 March attack by 748 heavies was aborted because of bad weather and seventy-nine bombers attacked targets of opportunity at Wilhelmshaven. Next day 4 March, the heavies were briefed to bomb Berlin again but bad weather forced the B-24s to abort early, leaving 502 Fortresses and 770 fighters to continue to the target.

B-17G-75-BO 43-37926 *Lotta Stern* whose nose art was inspired by the 'Varga girls' (pictures of female nudes by the Peruvian émigré Alberto Vargas) which adorned the back cover of the May 1944 Military Edition of *Esquire* magazine, was assigned overseas on 6 July 1944 and was assigned to the 490th Bomb Group but it spent most of its wartime career in the 100th Bomb Group before returning to the ZOI in July 1945. *(TAMM)*

Severe weather en route resulted in a recall and 219 B-17s hit targets of opportunity but the thirty B-17s in two squadrons in the 95th and one in the 100th did not receive the recall signal and continued to the capital alone. Fortunately, the Mustang escort was still with the wayward bombers and provided support in the target area. The P-51s prevented a debacle because 14 minutes from the capital, German fighters attacked them. The 95th lost four aircraft and the 100th, one which was *Seaton's Sad Sack*, piloted by Lieutenant Stanley M. Seaton (one KIA nine PoW), but the first American bombs had been dropped on Berlin. The 100th (and 95th) were later awarded a DUC. On 6 March the 8th dispatched 730 B-17s and B-24s and 801 escort fighters to targets in the suburbs of Berlin. The 3rd Bomb Division was assigned the Robert Bosch Electrical Equipment factory. The unprotected 13th Combat Bombardment Wing, comprising the 95th, 100th, and 390th Bomb Groups, caught the full venom of the enemy fighter attacks.

It was another black day for the 100th in particular, as Robert J. Shoens pilot of *Our Gal Sal* in the 351st Bomb Squadron, which flew lead relates:

I was part of 'Fireball Yellow', and the group was going with twenty planes; one short. It was a spectacular day, so clear it seemed we could almost see Berlin from over England. When we got home we found that we were one of only five B-17s to return to Thorpe Abbotts. We had lost fifteen airplanes. To say the least, we were upset, as was everyone on the base. Lieutenant Colonel Ollen 'Ollie' Turner, the 351st Bomb Squadron CO met us as we parked the airplane. He was in tears. Most of the losses had been from his squadron. It was hard to take, but this was what we had been trained for.

In fact in 30 minutes the enemy shot down twenty-three 13th Combat Bombardment Wing B-17s, or had damaged them so badly that they were forced to ditch or crash-land on the continent. The 3rd Bomb Division lost thirty-five B-17s, with the 'Bloody Hundredth' again suffering unmercifully at the hands of the *Luftwaffe*. The 8th lost a record sixty-nine bombers and eleven fighters, while 102 bombers were seriously damaged.

When the group was ordered back to Berlin within 24 hours they could have been forgiven if their nerve had cracked. Colonel John Bennett, who had taken over as Commanding Officer, led the 100th and all returned safely. The 3rd Bomb Division lost twenty-three Fortresses. Worst hit group in the 3rd Bomb Division during the series of Berlin missions was the 100th. On the first American operation to Berlin, on 4 March, the 'Bloody Hundredth' had won through to the target with the 95th while all the rest had turned back. On 8 March 600 bombers made the third raid on 'Big-B' in a week. The Third Division led the 8th to the VKF ball-bearing plant at Erkner in the suburbs east of Berlin. Thirty-seven Fortresses in the Third Division were shot down, including one in the 100th. It was for its '. . . outstanding performance of duty in action against the enemy in connection with the initial series of successful attacks against Berlin, 4, 6, and 8 March 1944. . . .' that the 100th was awarded its second Presidential Unit Citation, but not until 3 March 1945.

Hut in the snow at Thorpe Abbotts in the 1980s. *(Mike Fuenfer)*

In April Colonel Harding relinquished command of the 100th and Colonel Robert H. Kelly succeeded him. Kelly flew his first, and last, mission on 28 April, when the 100th was assigned a 'Noball' (V-1) site at Sottevast near Cherbourg. John A. Miller, right waist gunner in Lieutenant Larry Townsend's crew recalls:

At the morning's briefing our group CO, fresh from the States, told us, ''There'll be no evasive action when we're on the bomb run''. It was a beautiful day. We took off and soon we were starting on the bomb run. The flak was way below us as we made our run and there wasn't much of it. Then on the intercom I heard Townsend say that Kelly had called off the bomb drop and that we would have to go around again. We must have made the longest 360 in recorded history. Kelly took us far out over the water and it took forever. We came back in on the bomb run at the same speed, same altitude, and the same course, flying in rigid formation as Kelly ordered. The Kraut flak guns got us good! The *Kelly-Lakin* lead B-17 received two direct hits, one between the No. 2 engine and the cockpit and the second back toward the tail position. The plane disintegrated and fell to earth. Colonel Kelly was killed. A second Fortress, flown by Lieutenant

James W. McGuire, had its number one engine knocked from its mounting. The engine landed back on the left wing, setting it on fire. As he dived out of formation the left wing snapped off and the plane tumbled, a ball of fire, into the clouds below. The way that B-17 went down, the gyrations, how could a bombardier, of all people, get out and live to tell about it? But he did. John Jones, wherever you are, you're a walking miracle! I did not see any other 'chutes. (Six of the crew shared our hut with us in the 349th Squadron and all were KIA). The flak over Sottevast was unbelievably accurate! Every plane received hits and damage. Bernard Palmquist, ball gunner on Ralph W. Wright's crew, was hit, the flak going through his shoulder. He told me later that he had never seen such flak. This was the only time he could actually smell it. (Palmquist was still in hospital on 7 May when we started out for Berlin. Just as we were leaving England I watched the old B-17 his crew were flying dive out of formation. Somehow the flares, carried in the passageway to the nose, had exploded. All of Palmquist's officers were burned to death. The gunners baled out after much trouble.) When we returned to Thorpe Abbotts we were one shook-up bunch of fliers. At interrogation we told our story about the milk-run Colonel Kelly had chosen for his first mission with us. The intelligence interrogators were awed and amazed. One was heard to say, 'Colonel Kelly hasn't even unpacked yet'.

Colonel Thomas S. Jeffrey assumed command of the 100th in May (remaining in command until February 1945). On 19 May 888 B-17s and B-24s were dispatched, the B-17s attacking targets at Berlin and Kiel. Fighter opposition was heavy and twenty-eight bombers FTR. Three of them came from the 100th. Clarence F. Cherry, left waist gunner in Rogers Raiders piloted by Julian Rogers, recalls:

We left Thorpe Abbotts before daylight on 19 May 1944. Our flight was to Berlin. We were hit with light to mild flak over the target. So we thought we had a good flight. On our way back over Denmark we were flying low squadron and 'tail-end Charlie' position when we were attacked by Me 109s and

Fw 190s. They made about six passes at our position before my left waist position gun was completely blown out and I was wounded in the head. They removed me to the radio room for aid. They began to throw out equipment to lighten the ship. Already, two engines were gone. Finally, the pilot, Julian P. Rogers, told our crew to prepare to ditch in the sea. We made a rough landing. They threw me out of the top window in the radio room and I came out on the wing and started to float away from our sinking Fortress. They pulled me into the life raft. It was shot with cannon holes. We were close to two islands off Denmark. We could hear the small engines on the boats in the harbour. Julian said to us: 'Row out to sea'. We were not going to be PoWs. I don't know how far we rowed. Later on a Fortress came low and made a fix on our position. Some 40 hours later an RAF Lockheed ASR aircraft came over us and dropped a smoke flare on the water for wind drift. They dropped a wooden boat which had three parachutes attached to it. It dropped very close to us in the sea. We climbed aboard and started towards England. We ran into two Danish fishing boats and they interned us on their boat. They were going to take us back to Denmark as PoWs, but the British flying above us told them to stay put or be sunk. An ASR launch was on its way for us. We were taken to Great Yarmouth Hospital. All my crew was saved. I stayed at Great Yarmouth hospital for a few days and then went back to flying and completed my tour.

By 19 May 1944 17 year old gunner John A. Miller, who had flown the first Berlin mission, and who completed the most Berlin missions in one tour (six) by an 8th Air Force member, recalls:

Altogether, we started out for Berlin seven times. Twice our co-pilot went nuts and tried to crash us into the sea. These times the crew fought him off the wheel and we aborted. After the second time he didn't return to our crew. He wasn't a coward; he just couldn't go back to Berlin.

On 11 July 1944, the 100th had just returned from a mission to Munich when a burst of machine-gun fire was heard at Thorpe Abbotts. A machine gun in the ball turret of *She Hasta*

Although this mission list was photographed in a Nissen hut re-erected at a farm near Thorpe Abbotts it did not come from the 100th Bomb Group. *(Author)*

had started firing while the gunner, Sergeant Homer Parish was removing the guns for cleaning. As the gun fired, the turret revolved, spraying the surrounding area with bullets. Staff in the control tower sought the safety of the floor and three aircraft were damaged. Parish ran for cover but was caught in the gunfire and he was killed. *King Bee II*, which had been with 351st Bomb Squadron since late 1943, caught fire and though quickly extinguished the B-17 was only fit for scrap. One bullet penetrated the wall of Rectory farmhouse, a mile away, narrowly missing farmer Walter Brown who was sitting on a chair.

August and September 1944 saw the Fortresses bombing airfields in France and strategic targets in Germany. In mid-September the Fortresses flew a mercy drop to beleaguered Poles of the Polish Home Army in the ruins of Warsaw. The supply drop was made from between 13,000 and 18,000ft amid limited but accurate flak. The aircraft reached their shuttle base at Mirgorod and Poltava. On 19 September they took off again for the now familiar return flight via Italy and France, but this time without bombing because all French territory had been overrun. Bad weather throughout the rest of September severely limited missions, and only fourteen were flown that month. A mission to the refineries at Merseberg was flown on 11 September and the 100th put up thirty-six Forts. During assembly *Now An Then*, piloted by

Ron Batley (left) points out the Courage Rooster bar-tap to Mike Faley, 100th Bomb Group Historian from Studio City, California. This cast-metal rooster was given to Master Sergeant Bob Spangler, a line chief in the 351st Bomb Squadron after it was 'acquired' by one of the GIs during a night out in a local pub. Bob kept it for fifty years before returning it to Thorpe Abbotts. *(Author)*

Lieutenant Ferdinand J. Herres, suffered an engine fire and the crew baled out before the Fort crashed and burned on the Isle of Sheppey. Over Germany, an estimated 500 *Luftwaffe* fighters attacked and twelve B-17s including nine in the 350th Bomb Squadron were shot down. Lieutenant Cecil Daniels, who aborted just before the attack, reached the Allied lines near Paris but the B-17 was only fit for scrap.

On Saturday 30 September the 'Century Bombers' were stood down for two days as the base celebrated the Group's 200-mission party. Around 1,500 women from the services and civilian girls from as far afield as London, Newmarket, Norwich, and Ipswich, joined in the carnival atmosphere and dancing lasted until 0130 hours on Sunday morning. Days later women were still being combed from buildings. On 2 October it was back to the war and missions to France and Germany continued as V-2s began falling in eastern England and buzz bombs flew overhead. In November the 100th began operations with the B-17G, which was fitted with a chin turret for greater defence from frontal attack. As time went on, the older B-17F models gradually disappeared. Two that survived completed fifty missions and were returned to the United States. *Squawkin Hawk* bore the signatures of 349th Bomb Squadron personnel as well as those of local well wishers, while *Messie Bessie* had survived many missions as well as the indignity of having its landing gear retracted while at dispersal.

December 1944 brought the worst winter weather in England for 54 years. On New Year's Eve 1944, when 3rd Bomb Division crews returned to oil production centres, Hamburg became the scene of another disaster for the 100th when twelve B-17s failed to return. *Fools Rush In*, piloted by Lieutenant Floyd E. Henderson, was hit by flak on the bomb run and collided with 43-38124 flown by Lieutenant Clifton M. Williams, which also went down in flames. Only three men in each crew survived. 43-38215 flown by Lieutenant Billy C. Blackman, whose 418th Bomb Squadron crew was on their 13th mission, was hit by flak and the Fortress went down. Four crew were killed. 2nd Lieutenant William B. Sterrett, the navigator, and four others, including Blackman, who was blown out of the nose of the B-17 when it exploded, survived

and all became prisoners of war. 42-107233 flown by Lieutenant Wallace G. Wilson went down also but all nine crew survived. 43-38381 piloted by 2nd Lieutenant William Mayo, went down with the loss of all nine crew. 42-31895 flown by 2nd Lieutenant Paul L. Carroll was shot down and all nine crew were made PoW. 43-38459, flown by John Morin, was crash-landed near Emden. 43-38436, piloted by Lieutenant

100th Bomb Group Historian Mike Faley points out where Frank Valesh came to grief. The tree still bears the marks left by the B-17. (*Author*)

Rubble clearance at Thorpe Abbotts. *(Author)*

Charles C. Webster, went down with the loss of four men KIA including the two pilots. 43-38535, piloted by 2nd Lieutenant Ralph A. Whitcomb, was hit after the target and went spinning down in flames. *Faithful Forever* flown by Lieutenant Leo D. Ross also went down in a tight spin, though all nine crew got out safely. When Webster's B-17 was hit and left the formation in flames 1st Lieutenant Glenn H. Rojohn, pilot of *The Little Skipper*, manoeuvred to take over the slot left vacant. He was moving over when he experienced a 'tremendous impact'. Feeling the bomber shudder, the crew immediately thought their B-17 had collided with another aircraft. This was the case. 43-38457, flown by 1st Lieutenant William O. McNab and 2nd Lieutenant Nelson B. Vaughan had surged upwards and the top turret-guns on this bomber had pierced the skin on Rojohn's B-17 to bind both together. A fire now broke out in one of McNab's engines. Rojohn ordered co-pilot 2nd Lieutenant William O. Leek Jr. to bale out. Leek knew that Rojohn would never be able to maintain control by himself and would never survive the death spiral that would develop before he could get to the escape hatch. Accordingly he refused. As the aircraft impacted at Tettens near Wilhelmshaven Rojohn's B-17 slid off its companion, which immediately exploded. The surviving B-17, alternately lifting up and slamming back into the ground finally came to a halt after its left wing sliced through a wooden building blowing it to pieces. Of the six men in Rojohn's crew who baled out, four survived. Four of the McNab crew also survived.

January 1945 marked the 8th's third year of operations and it seemed as if the end of the war was in sight. On 19 January poor flying weather was responsible for the crew of *Heaven Can Wait* becoming lost in fog at Thorpe Abbotts. (On an earlier mission, the B-17 had returned with the tail gunner badly injured as a result of a bomb from another aircraft hitting and becoming wedged in the gunner's compartment). Lieutenant William Appleton crash landed with a full bomb load, skidded over the dispersal area to the east of the tower, crossed the road and came to rest in the field to the rear of the tower. Fortunately, dispersal ten was deserted, as were the tents nearby, which were demolished. As the crew of *Heaven Can Wait* scrambled to safety, the Fort began to burn. The area was cleared before the bomb load exploded and when the explosion occurred there were no injuries but there was much glass replacing to do, including the tower windows. Brick-Kiln Cottage nearby lost its windows and the ceilings were brought down. There was little left at the point of impact. *Heaven Can Wait* disintegrated and debris was scattered far and wide. One engine was hurled onto the airfield and came to rest beneath the tail of a parked B-17.

Despite the losses suffered during its tour of missions, a number of Forts flew 100 missions or more. *Fever Beaver* flew the most with 125 missions. *Our Gal Sal* and *Skipper II* each reached the 100 mark in March 1945, as did 42-97126. *Silver Dollar* completed 102 missions, but having survived all that the enemy could muster, was badly damaged in a taxiing accident. The B-17 was repaired and following a request from former Commanding Officer, Colonel Jeffrey, who had moved to a post in Germany, *Silver Dollar* was stripped of armament and it became his personal plane. As Jeffrey remarked, 'She was probably the last square D to be seen over Germany'. Despite losing a stabilizer over Germany to flak, *Gold Brick* was repaired and flown home to the States having notched up 100 missions. Fletcher's *Castoria* probably reached the 100-mission mark also. Original pilot Lieutenant William Fletcher was shot down in another B-17 in February 1944 but the *Castoria* survived to the end of the war. *Superstitious Aloysius* completed possibly 100 missions, while

Quittin Time (derived from the last three digits of 42-31530, the serial number) and 42-31991 also had a record of long service with the group.

During the week 18–25 April 1945; missions were briefed and scrubbed almost simultaneously as the ground forces overrun objective after objective. During the first week of May the German armies surrendered one by one. Starting on 1 May, before the Germans surrendered, Fortress crews flew mercy missions, called 'Chowhound', to starving Dutch civilians in Holland until the end of hostilities, carrying food. Bill Carleton, 351st Bomb Squadron Engineering Officer, recalls.

We flew three or four mercy missions to Holland until the end of hostilities, carrying food. One of them was before the Germans surrendered. They had promised us a corridor to fly across the country unmolested at low level. We could see German troops marching around in their black uniforms with swastikas flying. Our second mercy mission was on 5 May, the day the Germans in Holland surrendered. We went in at 200ft, buzzing a small sailboat on the Zeider Zee and blowing it over. We had orders not to drop unless we saw crowds of civilians, but the Dutch were lined up around the edges of the field waving and cheering. They had really turned out. Flags were flying everywhere and the streets were packed with people waving and cheering. It was a great day for the Dutch. We dropped our 4,000lb of food after trouble with the improvised 'drop doors' in the bomb bay. We buzzed Amsterdam a couple of times. Over the inter-phone came the call, 'Church steeple coming in at 12 o'clock high!' A little Dutch boy looked up and tried to race us on his bicycle. There were planes ahead of us who made their drops and people were running across the target area to get the food, unmindful of the fact that they could be knocked to Kingdom Come with a can of Spam. Planes all around us were starting to drop their food but our plane flew across the field without any salvo. The bombardier had gone to sleep! He awoke with a jerk and made the drop into the Zuider Zee. Such folly, but how typical. The best of intentions, the worst in execution. I hoped the forthcoming peace would be better than that!

The sixth and final 8th Air Force 'Chowhound' mission was flown on 7 May 1945, the day before VE (Victory in Europe) Day. Bill Carleton concludes:

> The 100th Bomb Group was known throughout the land not because we were superhuman but rather because we were human. Our fame and notoriety spread not just because of Regensburg or Berlin, but also because of our losses, and yes, even because of our *faux pas*. We were famous and to some of the new flyers, infamous both for what we did and what we gave. Mighty as we were, we were but a small fraction of the total force ultimately applied against the Axis Powers. We contributed our part and it was our knowledge and belief that others were making an even greater sacrifice that assured us of ultimate victory.

The Hundredth's departure left a void in many Norfolk people's lives. Billy Taylor, a schoolboy who lived with his parents in Upper Billingford in a house sandwiched between the petrol store and hardstand 3, carried on as normal, visiting the base for several days before the penny dropped.

The atmosphere was ghostly, building doors left open, some furniture still left in situation, curtains blowing in the wind, ashes in the tortoise stoves. Magazines on the floor, roadways deserted, the hospital empty; nothing remained alive ... Daily we visited our old haunts, the control tower, the fire station, where a few weeks earlier we had enjoyed coffee and eggs. All was silent. We walked the whole airfield hoping we were wrong; they would be back. Alas, it was not to be. Realization eventually came but still we visited our beloved Thorpe Abbotts.

Summary of Airfields and Other Locations

BURY ST EDMUNDS (ROUGHAM) – STATION 468

Description: American bomber base used by the 94th Bomb Group.
Location: 2 miles east of Bury St. Edmunds on A14.
Directions: Watch for sign for Rougham Industrial Estate and follow signs for the control tower. For Flying Fortress pub, continue on minor road off A14, ignoring road at left to technical site.
Comments: In the town centre of Bury St Edmunds is the Old English Rose Garden located in the Abbey grounds which pays homage to those lost in service with the 94th Bomb Group in WW2. At the entrance is a plaque reading:

> The construction of this old English rose garden is due to the generosity of an American friend of this borough Mr. John Appleby, who was stationed near Bury St. Edmunds during the war whilst a member of the United States Eighth Air Force. Mr Appleby became very attached to this old town and its historic associations and also to the surrounding countryside with its numerous picturesque villages and fine churches. His regard and affection for this portion of England

and its people is portrayed in his book *Suffolk Summer* written after his return to the United States. The Royalties from the sales of this book have been generously given to the Borough for making and effecting improvements to this Rose Garden.

Inside the garden is a memorial to the '94th Bombardment Group, Squadrons 331st, 332nd, 333rd, 410th and supporting units US Army Air Forces, 15 October 1977'. A B-17 is illustrated as well as the star-and-bars insignia of the USAAF. A second plaque reads: 'Presented to the people of Bury St Edmunds, a memorial honouring those men of the 94th Bombardment Group who gave their lives during World War II. 4th Combat Bombardment Wing, 8th Air Force, Rougham Airfield, Bury St Edmunds, 1943–1945'.

Also in the garden are three memorial seats, one of which is of aircraft alloy from a B-17 and inscribed: '1945 Presented to the City of Bury St Edmunds by the US Army Air Forces'. The others are wooden and were presented by the 94th Bomb Group Memorial Association and the 364th Fighter Group, which was based at Honington in 1944–45.

The control tower, which became a permanent dwelling 1945–1983 and was known as Tower House, is now the Museum. The Rougham Tower Association was formed by a group of local people in July 1993 with the aim of restoring the airfield control tower to its original condition. The Association became a Registered Charity in 1998. Entrance to the museum is free, except on event days. The museum is open every Sunday from the first Sunday in May until the last Sunday in October, normally between 11am and 4pm. Other times by appointment. During your visit you will be able to see what progress has been made to date and learn a little of the history of the Association and the Tower itself. To Join The Rougham Tower Association contact The Secretary, Rougham Tower Association, The Control Tower, Rougham Industrial Estate, Bury St Edmunds, Suffolk, P30 9XA. You will receive a quarterly newsletter *Rougham Roundup* plus discount on items purchased in the PX shop. Tel: 01359-271471 Fax 01449-737136. Email: tower@rougham.org website: www.rougham.org For Airfield Events see www.roughamairfield.org or Tel: 01359 270238.

On unclassified road 2 miles E of Bury St Edmunds is The Flying Fortress public house, which opened in December 1988 on the edge of the former airfield, featuring a B-17 on its sign. The refurbished building was previously a farm manager's house and during the war was used by the USAAF as the HQ of a ground unit. The car park is part of the old perimeter track.

CARLTON COLVILLE

Description: Site of a 487th Bomb Group B-17 crash.
Location: South of Lowestoft.
Directions: On B1384 A12 and A146.
Comments: On 14 March 1945 the bravery shown by 2nd Lieutenant Robert H. Portsch (24), a B-17G pilot in the 836th Bomb Squadron, 487th Bomb Group, saved Lowestoft from tragedy. Portsch's B-17 was one of thirty-six that took off from Lavenham for Hannover but when the No. 2 engine lost power over Belgium he was forced to abort the mission. Portsch crossed Lowestoft at 1450 hours when the engine suddenly exploded into flames. The burning bomber, loaded with HE bombs and incendiary containers began a wide circle to the left, back toward the open sea. Parachutes were seen descending as the crew began to abandon the aircraft. The tail gunner finished up hanging from a lamp post in Victoria Road, Oulton Broad. The last crewman jumped safely. He related how, when last seen, his pilot had been calmly going through the procedure to set the autopilot, so that he too could bale out. The flaming bomber was by now heading for the coast, where it was hoped that it would crash harmlessly into the sea but it rolled over and dived into a row of anti-tank blocks near Grove Farm, Carlton Colville, where it exploded into a blazing fireball. No one on the ground was injured but if the fuel and bomb-laden Fortress had crashed on the town itself, the outcome might have been different. Betty Larkin, 72, of Lowestoft Road, witnessed the crash. 'It just missed the houses, which was miraculous. That is why we are so thankful'. The body of Robert Portsch was found in a tree near the wreckage. He had managed to jump at the last moment, but was too low for his parachute to save him. As his radio operator jumped he hit the tail unit and fell in Dell Road without his parachute opening.

In 1986 workmen laying the footings for houses on what has since become Saxon Fields Estate, unearthed the wreckage of the wartime bomber from its resting place in a filled-in anti-tank trench. Numerous items, including a complete engine and propeller blades, were recovered and these can now be seen displayed at the Norfolk and Suffolk Aviation Museum at Flixton, near Bungay. Five roads on the Saxon Fields Estate have been named in honour of Portsch's crew on this fateful day. They include 'Fortress Road' and 'Portsch Close'. In December 1992 a memorial was unveiled at the site. The memorial plaque was the brainchild of Betty Larkin's husband Cyril (76) and his twin brother Claude erected the plinth.

DEBACH – STATION 152

Description: American bomber base used by the 493rd Bomb Group.
Location: Debach is 3 miles north-west of Woodbridge, Suffolk on unclassified road off B1078. Some of the sites were located in the adjoining village of Burgh.
Directions: Turn off the B1078 by Grove Farm in Clopton. Turn 1st right onto Snipe Road. 1st left will lead to the 493rd Bomb Group memorial. Clopton Church is on the B1079.
Comments: The 493rd Bomb Group memorial, as well as the memorial in Clopton Church and the Debach village sign, which bears a plaque dedicated to the 493rd Bomb Group, are well worth seeking out. The control tower is now the 493rd Bomb Group Museum. Contact Mr Richard Taylor, Grove Farm, Clopton, Woodbridge, Suffolk IP13 6QS at Web address www. 493gdebach.co.uk or email richard@prilly.fsnet.co.uk. Telephone 01473-737236. Information can also be obtained for hangar dance events. The museum is open on the last Sunday in the month from June to September 11am to 4pm.

DEOPHAM GREEN – STATION 142

Description: American bomber base used by the 452nd Bomb Group.
Location: 1¼ miles north of Attleborough, Norfolk, which is on the A11 Thetford to Norwich road.
Directions: Taking the A12 near Woodbridge turn left on to B1079. Pass Grundisburgh and Clopton and bear right on to B1078 to Clopton Corner. Entrance to airfield is further on, at right.
Comments: A Brick pillar with engraved map of airfield can be found on the intersection of the old runways. It has the inscription:

'February 1944–April 1945. Deopham Green, from this airfield 250 missions were flown by the 452nd Bomb Group (H). This memorial commemorates all those who served here. Dedicated 15 May 1992'.

Outside St Andrews Church in Hingham is a plaque by the war memorial which is inscribed: 'Memorial dedicated to the men of the 452nd Bomb Group (H) who sacrificed their lives in World War II that the ideals of democracy might live'.

ELVEDEN HALL (3RD AIR DIVISION HQ)

Description: Former HQ Third Bomb/Air Division (not open to the public).
Location: 4 miles south-east of Thetford, Norfolk on A11.
Directions: Pull off the A11 Elveden village into lay-by opposite the church.
Comments: A mansion in parkland by the A11 once owned by Maharajah Duleep Singh who in 1849 resigned his sovereign rights and property in India (including the Koh-I-Noor diamond) to the British Crown in exchange for a pension. With money from the British Government he purchased the 17,000 acre Elveden Estate in 1863. It allowed him to live the life of a country gentleman and follow his sporting interests and the 'Black prince' became a familiar name in the Thetford area. Between 1863 and 1870 with the help of the architect John Norton, he enlarged the hall into an Oriental extravaganza unparalleled in England. The walls, pillars and arches of the central domed hall were covered with intricate Indian ornamentation, all in white Carrara marble, the doors with panels of beaten copper. The Maharajah died in Paris in 1893. Lord Iveagh purchased Elveden in 1894 and he made even grander additions. Closer inspection reveals a huge copper dome on the roof and a massive Ionic portico and the stables. During the war the hall was the Headquarters of the 3rd Air Division, Eighth Bomber Command and periodically, home to two generals (Curtis E. LeMay and Frederick L. Anderson), fourteen colonels and 184 officers. The stables were converted into airmen's quarters. Inside the massive marble hall, the carved staircase was protected by plywood, while the Countess's boudoir was converted into a War Room with an Operations Room next door. Overlooking the park a vast dining room glittered with

chandeliers. Above were offices, lounges and bedrooms. Lord Iveagh opened his park for the Americans, including a part to shoot over with his gamekeeper. There were baseball and football matches, and firm friendships developed with the locals in the pubs and at the hops in the village hall. Lord Iveagh was killed in the Normandy landings.

Inside St Andrew and St Patrick's Elveden village church, approached from the direction of the hall by a beautiful cloister, or from the front stone porch, a stained glass window, the work of British artist, Hugh Easton, doyen of the creators of airmen's memorial windows, depicts an unknown young airman kneeling humbly beneath the wings of an angel. One pair of the angel's wings are spread out, one pair enfold the airman, lightly resting on his shoulder. Beyond are the hangars and the American aircraft at their dispersal under the shade of British oaks. The window was unveiled on 8 January 1947. There is an inscription: 'In honour and memory of the members of the Third Air Division who, based in Britain, fell while on air operations in the war of freedom 1942–1945. Mundis libris'. The church is kept locked but you can ring Brandon Rectory on 01842-811907.

EYE (BROME) – STATION 134

Description: American bomber base used by the 490th Bomb Group.
Location: 11 miles from Stowmarket, Suffolk.
Directions: Parallel to the A140 Norwich to Ipswich road just after Scole.
Comments: Lychgate and plaques on wall adjacent to church of St Peter and St Paul in Eye.

FERSFIELD (WINFARTHING) – STATION 554, (FORMERLY 140)

Description: Satellite base used by the 388th Bomb Group for 'Aphrodite' missions.
Location: 3 miles north of the A1066 Thetford–Diss road in Norfolk.
Directions: From Diss the airfield can be approached either from the A1066 Thetford–Diss road or from the B1077 Shelfanger Road northwards out of the town sign-posted Shelfanger.

Comments: Significant lengths of all three runways remain plus the entire perimeter track although its width has also been reduced. Also present is one of the original hangars plus a number of derelict camp buildings.

FRAMLINGHAM (PARHAM) – STATION 153

Description: American bomber base used by the 390th Bomb Group.
Location: 3 miles from Framlingham on unclassified road off A12 in Suffolk.
Directions: Situated one mile south-west of Great Glemham east of the B1116 (Hacheston-Framlingham Road). Turn off through Parham village or turn off the A12 directly opposite Glemham Hall.
Comments: In 1976 following 31 years of neglect, a small group of aircraft enthusiasts began the five-year restoration of the control tower. When completed the tower was dedicated in a formal ceremony in 1981. The tower and surrounding buildings for the Parham Airfield Memorial Museum and the Museum of the British Resistance Organisation – the Auxiliary Units, opened in 1997. The latter is the only museum in the UK dedicated to all the men and women who served in the various sections of the highly secret Auxiliary Units, or underground resistance network. For more information see www.parhamairfieldmuseum.co.uk or telephone 01728-621373. The Museum is open Sundays and Bank Holiday Mondays from the first Sunday in March to the last Sunday in October between 11am and 5pm. During June, July, August and September the Museum is open Wednesdays from 11am to 4pm. Admission is free. Visits outside these hours can only be made by contacting the Museum and arranging an appointment. This may incur a charge. There is ample car parking, a souvenir shop and light refreshments are available. There is also a Picnic Area.

A plaque on the wall of the former control tower reads: 'This memorial honours the men of the 390th Bomb Group (H) who gave their lives during the period 1943–1945, operating from Station 153, Parham. Dedicated May 1981'. The tower houses a museum dedicated to the 390th Bomb Group. A bungalow built on the edge of the old airfield at Crabbes Farm is named 'Moller's

Piece' after Colonel Joseph A. Moller, the CO of the 390th from 1944 to the end of the war, and is a personal tribute by the owner of the farm, Mr Percy Kindred.

GREAT ASHFIELD – STATION 155

Description: American bomber base used by the 385th Bomb Group.

Location: 5 miles north-west of Stowmarket, Suffolk and about 10 miles east of Bury St. Edmunds and 3 miles north of the A14 at Elmswell.

Directions: 4–5 miles past Stowmarket, take exit for A1088 and immediately go right on to minor road through Elmswell and over railway level crossing, continuing north. Turn right into lane to Lea Farm after water tower. For the church, do not turn but go straight on to Great Ashfield.

Comments: In the village churchyard of All Saints Church is a memorial bearing the inscription: 'In memoriam of the officers and men of the 385th Heavy Bombardment Group US Army Air Force who gave their lives in the air battles over Europe 1943–1944. This plaque is placed here by the comrades of those men as an everlasting tribute to their heroic sacrifice and unselfish devotion to duty'. The plaque was sited outside the HQ building at Great Ashfield as early as 1944. A memorial altar can be found in the north aisle of the church as well as the 385th's Roll of Honour, a book containing the names of all those killed in action. A stained glass window next to the American Memorial Altar commemorates those who lost their lives while stationed at Great Ashfield. It depicts the sky with aircraft and a dove for peace, as well as the three trees, which were the landmark on the airfield for returning aircraft.

HONINGTON – STATION 375

Description: American bomber base used by the 1st SAD.

Location: On unclassified road off A1088, in Suffolk, 7 miles from Bury St. Edmunds.

Directions: Take B1106, on seeing 'RAF Honington' sign at roundabout and go through Fornham All saints to A134, then turn left. Travel for 5 miles until next RAF Honington sign, then turn right into minor road. RAF station is on the left.

Comments: Outside the Guardroom of this RAF station is a dwarf brick wall on which are plaques honouring the 364th Fighter Group which flew Lightnings and Mustangs from here between February 1944 and November 1945. Just outside the main gate is a second memorial, bearing the inscription: 'Eighth Air Force USAAF. In memory of the men of the 1st Strategic Air Depot RAF Honington AAF595 1942–1946. Never forgotten, forever honoured. Dedicated 26 September 1987'.

HORHAM – STATION 119

Description: American bomber base used by the 95th Bomb Group.
Location: On B1117, 6 miles from Eye.
Directions: to find the Hospital museum, turn off the B1117 about 3 miles east of Eye, on sharp bend. Museum is on the left after about ¼ mile.
Comments: Near the village church the stone silhouette of a B-17 fin and rudder overshadows a plan view of Horham's runways on a flat base beneath. On one side of the fin is the 'Square B' symbol of the 95th Bomb Group. On the other is a plaque with the unit badge and inscription: 'In memory of the men of the 95th Bombardment Group who served at Horham airfield and to those who gave their lives in the cause of freedom, 1943–1945. 334th, 335th, 336th and 412th Bomb Squadrons and supporting units, Headquarters 13th Combat Bomb Wing, United States 8th Air Force. Dedicated 19th Sept. 1981.'

A visit to the unique Red Feather Club, originally the NCOs' mess, now fully restored by a small group of enthusiasts, and the former base hospital which is now the 95th BG (H) Hospital Museum, are a must. The 95th BG Heritage Association has restored the bar area in the Red Feather Club whose walls are covered in beautiful wartime murals painted by Nathan Bindler. The Red Feather Club has open days throughout the year. (Contact Frank Sherman on 01379 678471 or Alan Johnson on 01379 384472) www.95thbg-horham.com. For the Hospital Museum contact Mr Tony Albrow on 01379 870514, and www. 95thbghosiptalmuseum.co.uk. Opening times by appointment. Admission free. Donations welcome.

Stradbroke church also has strong connections with Horham airfield.

IPSWICH

Description: Liberty town in Suffolk during WWII.
Location: Off the A140/A12 in Suffolk.
Directions: Turn off A140/A12 bypass and follow signs.
Comments: In 1602 Bartholomew Gosnold from Otley near Ipswich led an exploratory expedition of eighty-two men aboard *Concord* to the coast of what was then called 'the north parts of Virginia'. He duly made landfall in the vicinity of Cape Cod and explored the area, naming Martha's Vineyard, either after his wife's mother or in memory of his daughter of that name who had recently died. Five years later Gosnold returned with a larger party to create the first permanent settlement from England in the New World. This settlement was not however in New England but at Jamestown in (modern) Virginia. The change of destination is an unsolved puzzle. Whatever the reason, it is noteworthy that not far from Jamestown is a city called Suffolk, together with the larger city of Norfolk. Visitors to his birthplace, Otley Hall, have the opportunity to learn more about his exploits. In 1610 the Borough of Ipswich bought four shares in the Virginia Company which financed voyages to America. A preacher called Nathaniel Ward, who came from Haverhill, which has also given its name to a town in Massachusetts, emigrated to Massachusetts and renamed the small community of Agarram as Ipswich.

In WW2 Ipswich in Suffolk was a 'liberty town' for servicemen and women but which according to *Ipswich Evenings,* in *Here We Are Together* by Robert S. Arbib Jr., 'could not have been farther removed from that Dickensian world than Ipswich in the autumn and winter of 1942. Dirty, crowded, noisy, evil smelling, it was then a composite of the smaller English provincial metropolis at war. Though it retained to some degree its basic East Anglian character, it was now in addition a roaring industrial town, a busy port and an amusement centre for troops of a dozen Allied nations. Nine miles from our camp at Debach, it became the destination for most of us on our weekly twenty-four-hour leaves and the source of many an evening's adventure. We thronged it, we criticised it and we admired it. We changed its life considerably. The first stop was the YMCA where GIs could shave and wash in hot water. Then they went upstairs and had breakfast for a few pennies. Coffee and hot buttered toast, with jam and a few pleasant words from the girl in slacks who worked behind the counter.

The liberty trucks from USAAF bases in the area parked in Princes Street and the GIs headed for cinemas, public houses (Ipswich boasted nearly 200 of these) such as The Cricketers, The Great White Horse, The Mulberry Tree, The Crown and Anchor, The Golden Lion, The Unicorn where the American would occasionally enjoy a quiet hour in less frantic surroundings, and the less-imposing Fox, The Plough, The Blue Coat Boy and The Waggon and Horses. There was a dance at Ipswich almost every night of the week, either at the Co-operative Hall or St. Lawrence's Church Hall. 'Perhaps the chief attraction of Ipswich', concludes Arbib, 'was the girls. It seemed to us then a town of girls, with a high proportion of young and pretty ones and their behaviour was nothing like that of girls we had known at home'. The liberty trucks left Princes Street at eleven and the ride home was an ordeal'.

KNETTISHALL – STATION 136

Description: American bomber base used by the 388th Bomb Group.
Location: Off unclassified road 1 mile North of Coney Weston, Suffolk, 6 miles south-east of Thetford.
Directions: At Stanton join B111 to Barningham. Join minor road north towards Knettishall. Memorial is at crossroads between Coney Weston and Hopton.
Comments: The main memorial here shows a head-on view of a B-17G breaking a symbolic chain of oppression. Beneath are two more B-17s in plan view and in 'missing man formation'. The inscription reads: 'United States Army Air Forces, 388th Bomb Group (H), RAF Knettishall Station 136, 23 June 1943–1945 August 1945. Fortress for freedom. 306 missions, 191 aircraft lost, 222 enemy aircraft destroyed, 8,051 sorties, 542 killed, 801 prisoners. In fond memory of those men of the 388th Bomb group (H) who, flying from this field, served with honour and died bravely in the cause of freedom. This memorial was dedicated on May 17 1986 by survivors of the 388 Bombardment Group (H).

LAVENHAM (COCKFIELD) – STATION 137

Description: American bomber base used by the 487th Bomb Group.

Location: On A1141, 3 miles from the town.

Directions: Leave the village taking the A1141 main Bury St Edmunds road and after 3 miles, turn left onto a narrow road signposted, 'Smithwood Green only'.

Comments: A plaque on the wall of the market place, unveiled on 2 August 1970, reads: 'Dedicated to the men of the 487th Bomb Group (H) who sacrificed their lives in World War II that the ideals of democracy might live'. An American flag hangs inside the church. On the old control tower at Lavenham airfield is a plaque inscribed: 'USAAF Station 137 Lavenham. 487th Bomb Group (H) were stationed here November 1943 to October 1945'. The plaque was dedicated on 10 May 1986.

In the Swan Hotel hangs a portrait of Brigadier General Fred Castle and the bar is flanked by RAF and USAAF/USAF memorabilia including some wartime signatures behind glass.

MENDLESHAM (WETHERINGSETT) – STATION 156

Description: American bomber base used by the 34th Bomb Group.

Location: 5¼ miles north-east of Stowmarket on the eastern side of the A140 Ipswich to Norwich main road. The flying field is situated at Wetherup Street whereas the living sites were on the western side of the A140 in the parish of Mendlesham.

Directions: For best views of the runways, turn off the A140, signed Park Green. There is memorial beside the A140 Ipswich–Norwich road. Near the Memorial there is a lay-by on the A140, which is where the memorial ought to be because you take your life in your hands if you are travelling by car and are trying to find it!

Comments: The poignant memorial for the 34th Bomb Group showing a pilot leaning out of a B-17 cockpit holding a laurel branch was erected in 1949 and the inscription reads: 'To the American Airmen of the '34th' who, in valor, gave their lives to the victory that made real the challenge for world peace and unity. The 34th Heavy Bombardment Group. A unit of the United States Eight Air Force in World War II, April 1944 to June 1945. Mendlesham Aerodrome, Suffolk. Henry Berg 49'. (Berg was a well-known Baltimore sculptor).

QUIDENHAM

Description: Village Church near Snetterton Heath with memorial stained glass window to the 96th Bomb Group.
Location: On unclassified road 1½ miles north-west of Kenninghall, Norfolk.
Directions: On minor road heading from Snetterton airfield to Kenninghall. If heading on A11 turn onto road for East Harling.

Wartime photo of an airman praying in the chapel at Quidenham. *(USAF)*

In the 14th century chapel in the south aisle of St Andrews Church is a stained glass window showing an airman, aircraft overhead, an angel and Unit badges with the motto, *E sempre l'ora*. It was subscribed by personnel of 96th Bomb Group at Snetterton Heath.

Comments: In the 14th century chapel in the south aisle of St Andrews Church is a stained glass window showing an airman, aircraft overhead, an angel and unit badges with the motto, *E sempre l'ora*. It was subscribed by personnel of 96th Bomb Group at Snetterton Heath and on the wall below is the inscription: 'Memorial Chapel. In memory of comrades who gave their lives in the cause of freedom. 1943–1945. 96th Bombardment Group (H). United States Army Air Forces'. The preliminary design for the window was conceived and drawn up by Sergeant Gerald Athey, an aircraft mechanic at Snetterton. Mr Reginald Bell of London, much of whose work can be seen in America, including some of the windows in the Cathedral Church of St John the Divine, New York, designed the stained glass. The Bishop of Norwich dedicated the chapel on 17 November 1944. A service of remembrance was held in the church on 30 May 1946 in memory of the men of the 8th Air Force who were killed in WWII. The service was broadcast to the USA and Richard Dimbleby described to the people of America, the beautiful memorial, the service and the scene in the church. A replica of this window is installed in the Memorial Chapel of the 8th Air Force Heritage Centre in Savannah, Georgia.

Eccles Hall School utilises some of the old Snetterton airfield buildings, including the former base hospital. A Nissen hut houses a small museum commemorating the 96th Bomb Group.

See also Snetterton Heath.

RATTLESDEN – STATION 126

Description: American bomber base used by the 447th Bomb Group.
Location: In Suffolk 3 miles south of the village of the same name.
Directions: On minor roads west of the B1115 from Stowmarket.
Comments: Four squadron badges, a head-on view of a B-17 and the 'Square K' symbol of the 447th Bomb Group appear on this memorial, along with the words: 'Dedicated to the members of the 447th Bomb Group and their supporting units in remembrance and gratitude of their fight in the cause of freedom from Rattlesden Airfield (Station 126) 1943–1945'. The memorial was dedicated on 3 June 1984. The wartime control tower was restored with the

sponsorship of 447th veterans and a plaque inside records this fact. The building is now the HQ of the Rattlesden Gliding Club.

SNETTERTON HEATH – STATION 138

Description: American bomber base used by the 96th Bomb Group.

Location: On the southern side of the A11, six miles south-west of Attleborough and 8 miles from Thetford in Norfolk on un-classified road 1 mile south-west of Snetterton village.

Directions: Parallel to the A11 after the Larling bypass and before Attleborough. Look for signs for racing circuit and Sunday markets.

Comments: It was like a 'dream come true' for Peder Larsen to go back to Snetterton and to see the people who had meant so much during the war. 'You become close to people very quickly when you're in a life and death situation. Now there are no planes on the hardstand at Snetterton Heath. The old runway is a racing circuit with the roar of racing cars and motorcycles replacing the roar of our engines as we lined up to take off on a mission. The living quarters have been demolished and that land is now used for farming. Only three bomb shelters remain. These were used when our field was strafed or when a buzz-bomb engine stopped overhead – it was then that we ran for cover! The motor pool building, the parachute rigging silo, the operations building and a pile of large timbers stored in the woods are all that remain of the old base. St Andrews Church meant a great deal to me during the war and also played an important part in our missions. On our return we knew when we saw the church steeple that we were almost home safe. Snetterton Heath echoes to the roars of racing cars and the cheers of crowds, but the volume of all that will never drown those two years 40 years ago'.

An impressive 30ft high stainless steel memorial monument is located beside the entrance to the motor racing circuit and symbolizes a V-17 climbing away on a mission. On the plinth is inscribed: 'Dedicated to all personnel of the 96th Bombardment Group (H), 8th USAAF, who served on this airfield 1944–1945'. It was dedicated in May 2002. The four columns are contrails, each increasing in size as they reach the ground representing the

support needed from each of the four squadrons to get the aircraft
ready for their bombing Missions.
See also Quidenham.

SUDBURY (ACTON) – STATION 174

Description: American bomber base used by the 486th Bomb
Group.
Location: between the villages of Great Waldingfield and Acton,
two miles north-east of Sudbury in Suffolk.
Directions: Turn off the A11 intersection, taking the slip road to
the Race Circuit and Sunday Market. Follow the old runway down
to the circuit entrance. The monument is on the left.
Comments: John Winthrop was another Suffolk man who contributed greatly to the development of New England. His family
lived for generations at the village of Groton, near Sudbury. In
1680 he emigrated to take charge of the Massachusetts Company,
founded the city of Boston and became first Governor of the State
of Massachusetts. He has been described as the 'Father of New
England' and is buried in Kings Chapel, Boston. One of his sons
(also John) became first Governor of Connecticut and a major city
in this state carries the name of the ancestral home located beside
the entrance to the motor racing circuit located beside the entrance
to the motor racing circuit, Groton. Thomas Davies, from Sudbury,
set the lantern in the tower of Old North Church, Boston, giving
the signal to Paul Revere to make his famous ride.
In Sudbury town centre is a Town Hall plaque bearing the
words: 'To the citizens of Sudbury for their fellowship, under-
standing and hospitality, from the officers and men of the 486th
Bombardment Group (H), 418 Air Services Group USAAF 1944–5'.
A granite memorial can be found outside St Gregory's church.
The design includes the Group's badge, illustrations of the B-17
and B-24 and an outline view of the airfield. The inscription
reads: '486th Bombardment Group (H). The 486th flew 191 combat
missions over Nazi held Europe from May 1944 to July 1945. This
memorial was dedicated by survivors of the 486th and the town
of Sudbury in honour of those who served and the 400 airmen
who died in the cause of freedom. Dedicated 4th July 1987.'
On the old Sudbury airfield is a stone with a plaque inscribed:
'In recognition of the USAAF 486th Bombardment Group (Heavy)

operating from this airfield between March 1944 and August 1945'. The hangars of the old airfield are now occupied by Ashdown Rawlinson Ltd, agricultural merchants. Only the base of the control tower remains but much of the perimeter track and hardstandings can still be seen in their original state although some material was been removed by St. Ives Sand & Gravel.

Thorpe Abbotts Memorial Museum – Station 139

Description: American bomber base used by the 100th Bomb Group.
Location: In Suffolk, 4 miles north-east of Diss near Dickleburgh off the A140.
Directions: Signposted from the A140 Dickleburgh bypass or the A143 Scole–Bungay road.
Comments: Thorpe Abbotts Tower Museum is one of the finest of its kind in East Anglia. In the mid-1970s Mike Harvey, who had been a boy when B-17s flew over his home, visited the deteriorating building which had once been the Flying Control Tower. He closed his eyes and recalled the throaty sound of Fortress engines and vowed that the memory of the airmen who flew from East Anglia would not be forgotten. Later Mike wrote, 'I decided it was a pity that the country of my birth couldn't do more to remember what the men of the USAAF had done during WW2. On making inquiries locally, I found there were a lot of people who shared my views. So the idea was born'. The project to restore the control tower and open it as a Memorial Museum began in earnest in September 1977 when a number of 100th Bomb Group Association veterans returned. The tower, like most of the remaining buildings, was in a derelict state and indeed as the group posed on the balcony for photographs there was doubt expressed as to the safety of the structure. The possibility of restoring the building was mentioned and during the following weeks Mike, his wife Jean, Paul Meen and Carol and Ron Batley, gathered to consider the idea. The two landlords, David Wigan and Sir Rupert Mann, owner of the tower gave permission for the building to be surveyed. Having proved that the structure was still sound, the group negotiated a 999 year lease and the long task of clearing the site and bringing the tower back to its original condition began. From then on the

group received help from a great number of local firms and individuals. Film shows, raffles and other money raisers provided much needed income. The 100th association in the United States donated generously from their funds and provided the interest and contacts without which the project could not have succeeded.

One of those involved in the restoration was Sam Hurry, a schoolboy in Diss in WWII. He recalls:

I was alone in the tower in the ground floor front room, at about 1:45pm, paint brush in hand. A breeze came through the room, then noises started, with aircraft engines, radios (RT) followed by men shouting. I was oblivious to anything else other than the noise, but I must say that prior to this, five minutes before, I had glanced out of the window and thought what a wonderful day it was. What seemed ages, was but a few seconds or so. I left the tower at 1:55pm and headed straight home. My wife Jane was surprised to see me home so early. I did not tell her at that time but did tell her later. Mike Harvey, Ron Batley and I have all experienced an unusual atmosphere at the tower prior to the dedication.

By May 1981 the restoration work had been completed and a plaque had been set in the wall near the main entrance. Major Horace Varian; secretary of the 100th association and formerly Group Adjutant unveiled the plaque at a ceremony of dedication on 25 May. From that date work has continued to create a museum, which tells the story of the 100th during their stay at Thorpe Abbotts. Many men based here during the war have contributed uniforms, equipment, decorations, photographs and combat records. On the ground floor of the tower museum there are exhibits that are of special interest; photos, uniforms armaments and a Chapel of Remembrance. While on the first floor are displayed photos, uniforms, medals and many interesting documents. There are also personal items from the men who served at Thorpe Abbotts 1943–45. The search for artifacts continues. (Donations should be sent to: 100th Bomb Group Memorial Museum, Common Road, Dickleburgh, Diss, Norfolk, England, IP21 4PH or fax 011-44-379-871-485.) Outbuildings house aircraft engines, office, tech supply, heavy oil engine, tyre shop, and a mock up of an accommodation area. The superb Horace L. Varian Centre, with its beautiful panoramic mural and a refreshment bar and museum shop, is the perfect visitor centre. The village church contains the US flag and Unit Citation. The museum is open Saturdays, Sundays, Bank Holidays, or by appointment (tel. 01379-740708) from 10am to 5 pm throughout the year. From May to September the Museum is also open on Wednesdays.

It is in no small part due to the efforts of the small group of enthusiasts and their sponsors that Thorpe Abbotts is a shining example of the airfield preservation movement in England today. This splendid museum epitomizes the character and history of what was and still is one of the most famous fields of Little America. It is also a fitting memorial to the over 700 men who did not return from missions flown from Thorpe Abbotts.

APPENDIX II

3rd Air Division
Order of Battle

Date	Group	Remarks
1943		
13 May	94th	Became Operational. St. Omer
	95th	Became Operational. St. Omer
	96th	Became Operational. St. Omer
22 June	100th	Mission debut. Diversion over North Sea
17 July	385th	Mission debut, Hannover
	388th	Mission debut, Hannover
12 August	390th	Mission debut. Ruhr Valley
24 December	447th	Became Operational. 'Noball' targets
1944		
5 February	452nd	Mission debut, Romilly
3 May	34th	Mission debut
7 May	486th	Mission debut
7 May	487th	Mission debut
7 May	490th	Mission debut
6 June	493rd	Mission debut
1 August	486th	1st mission after converting from B-24
1 August	487th	1st mission after converting from B-242
7 August	490th	1st mission after converting from B-24
8 September	493rd	1st mission after converting from B-241
7 September	34th	1st mission after converting from B-24

3rd Bomb/Air Division Combat Bombardment Wing Assignments: 1 November 1943

Group	Final Combat Bombardment Wing Assignment		Base
34th	93rd CBW	18.4.44–2.8.45	Mendlesham
94th	4th CBW	13.6.43–12.12.45	Rougham
95th	13th CBW	15.6.43–3.8.45	Horham
96th	45th CBW	12.6.43–11.12.45	Snetterton Heath
100th	13th CBW	9.6.43–11.12.45	Thorpe Abbotts
385th	4th CBW*	26.6.43–4.8.45	Great Ashfield
388th	45th CBW	23.6.43–5.8.45	Knettishall
390th	13th CBW	14.7.43–4.8.45	Framlingham
447th	4th CBW	30.11.43–2.8.45	Rattlesden
452nd	45th CBW	3.1.44–5.8.45	Deopham Green
486th	4th CBW	3.44–25.8.45	Sudbury (Acton)
487th	4th CBW	4.4.44–24.8.45	Lavenham
490th	93rd CBW	26.4.44–24.8.45	Eye (Brome)
493rd	93rd CBW	4.44–6.8.45	Debach

*93rd Combat Bombardment Wing from 17 February 1945

APPENDIX IV

3rd Bomb Division
Squadron Assignments

Group	Squadron	Squadron Code Letters
34th Bomb Group	4th Bomb Squadron	(Q6)
	7th Bomb Squadron	(R2)
	18th Bomb Squadron	(8I)
	391st Bomb Squadron	(3L)
94th Bomb Group	331st Bomb Squadron	(QE)
	332nd Bomb Squadron	(XM)
	333rd Bomb Squadron	(TS)
	410th Bomb Squadron	(GL)
95th Bomb Group	334th Bomb Squadron	(BG)
	335th Bomb Squadron	(OE)
	336th Bomb Squadron	(ET)
	412th Bomb Squadron	(QW)
96th Bomb Group	337th Bomb Squadron	(QJ)
	338th Bomb Squadron	(BX)
	339th Bomb Squadron	(AW)
	413th Bomb Squadron	(MZ)
100th Bomb Group	349th Bomb Squadron	(XR)
	350th Bomb Squadron	(LN)
	351st Bomb Squadron	(EP)
	418th Bomb Squadron	(LD)

Group	Squadron	Squadron Code Letters
385th Bomb Group	548th Bomb Squadron	(GX)
	549th Bomb Squadron	(XA)
	550th Bomb Squadron	(SG)
	551st Bomb Squadron	(HR)
388th Bomb Group	560th Bomb Squadron	
	561st Bomb Squadron	
	562nd Bomb Squadron	
	563rd Bomb Squadron	
390th Bomb Group	568th Bomb Squadron	(El)
	569th Bomb Squadron	(CC)
	570th Bomb Squadron	(DI)
	571st Bomb Squadron	(FC)
447th Bomb Group	708th Bomb Squadron	(CQ)
	709th Bomb Squadron	(IE)
	710th Bomb Squadron	(IJ)
	711th Bomb Squadron	(IR)
452nd Bomb Group	728th Bomb Squadron	(9Z)
	729th Bomb Squadron	(M3)
	730th Bomb Squadron	(6K)
	731st Bomb Squadron	(7D)
486th Bomb Group	832nd Bomb Squadron	(H8)
	833rd Bomb Squadron	(2S)
	834th Bomb Squadron	(3R)
	835th Bomb Squadron	(H8)
487th Bomb Group	836th Bomb Squadron	(RS)
	837th Bomb Squadron	(3C)
	838th Bomb Squadron	(3G)
	839th Bomb Squadron	(4F)
490th Bomb Group	848th Bomb Squadron	(7W)
	849th Bomb Squadron	(W8)
	850th Bomb Squadron	(7Q)
	851st Bomb Squadron	(S3)

Group	Squadron	Squadron Code Letters
493rd Bomb Group	860th Bomb Squadron	(N6)
	861st Bomb Squadron	(G6)
	862nd Bomb Squadron	(8M)
	863rd Bomb Squadron	(Q4)

Bibliography

Andrews, Paul M. & Adams, William H. *Heavy Bombers of the Mighty Eighth*. (Eighth Air Force Museum Foundation Project Bits & Pieces) 1995

Arbib Robert S. Jr., *Here We Are Together, The Notebook of an American Soldier in Britain*

Beaty David, *Light Perpetual: Aviators' Memorial Windows* (Airlife) 1995

Birdsall, Steve & Freeman, Roger A. *Claims to Fame – The B-17 Flying Fortress* (Arms & Armour) 1994

Birdsall, Steve. *Pride of Seattle – The Story of the first 300 B-17Fs* (Squadron Signal) 1998

Blakebrough, Ken, *The Fireball Outfit* (1968)

Bowden, Ray. *Plane Names & Fancy Noses – the 91st BG (H)* (Design Oracle Partnership) 1993

Bowman Martin W. *8th Air Force At War* (PSL) 1994

Bowman Martin W. *Airfield Focus 62: Thorpe Abbotts* (GMS 2003)

Bowman Martin W. *B-17 Flying Fortress Units of the Eighth Air Force (Part 2)* (Osprey) 2002

Bowman Martin W. *B-17 Groups of the Eighth Air Force in Focus* (Red Kite) 2004

Bowman Martin W. *Boeing B-17 Flying Fortress.* (Crowood) 1998

Bowman Martin W. *Castles In The Air* (PSL) 1984 (Red Kite) 2001

Bowman Martin W. *Combat Legends B-17 Flying Fortress* (Airlife) 2002

Bowman Martin W. *Echoes of East Anglia* (Halsgrove Publishing Ltd) 2006

Bowman Martin W. *Fields of Little America* (Wensum Books) 1977 (PSL) 1983, 1988 (GMS) 2001

Bowman Martin W. *Flying To Glory* (PSL) 1992

Bowman Martin W. *Four Miles High* (PSL) 1992

Bowman Martin W. *Great American Air Battles* (Airlife) 1994

Bowman Martin W. *Sentimental Journey* (Erskine Press) 2005

Bowman Martin W. *The B-24 Liberator* (Wensum Books) 1979 (PSL) 1989

Bowman Martin W. *The Bedford Triangle* (PSL) 1988, (Sutton) 1996, 2003

Bowman Martin W. *USAAF Handbook 1939–1945* (Sutton) 1997, 2003

Bowman Martin W. *Ghost Airfields of East Anglia* (Halsgrove Publishing Ltd) 2007

Bowyer, Michael J. F. *Action Stations 1: East Anglia* (PSL) 1990

Congdon, Philip *Behind the Hangar Doors* (Sonik)

Fairhead, Huby & Tuffen, Roy *Airfields & Airstrips of Norfolk & Suffolk* (Norfolk & Suffolk Aviation Museum)

Fairhead, Huby *Aeronautical Memorials of Suffolk* (Norfolk & Suffolk Aviation Museum) 1989

Fairhead, Huby *Aeronautical Memorials of Norfolk* (Norfolk & Suffolk Aviation Museum) 1995.

Francis, Paul *Military Airfield Architecture From Airships to the Jet Age* (PSL) 1996

Freeman, Roger A. *Airfields of the Eighth Then and Now* (After the Battle) 1978

Freeman, Roger A. *Mighty Eighth War Manual* (Jane's) 1984

Freeman, Roger A. *The Mighty Eighth* (MacDonald) 1970

Freeman, Roger A. *The Mighty Eighth In Art* (Arms & Armour) 1996

Freeman, Roger A. *The Mighty Eighth in Colour* (Arms & Armour) 1991

Freeman, Roger A. with Osborne, David. *The B-17 Flying Fortress Story* Arms & Armour, 1998

Hale, Edwin R. W. and Turner, John Frayn *The Yanks Are Coming* (Midas Books) 1983

Innes, Graham Buchan *British Airfield Buildings Expansion & Inter-War Periods* (Midland) 2000

Innes, Graham Buchan *British Airfield Buildings of the Second World War* (Midland) 1995

Lande D. A. *From Somewhere in England* (Airlife) 1991

Lay, Beirne Jr and Bartlett, Sy. *Twelve O'Clock High* (Ballatine Books) 1948

Marriott, Leo British *Military Airfields Then & Now* (Ian Allan Publishing) 1997

McDowell, Ernest R. *Flying Fortress in Action* (Squadron Signal) 1987

McKenzie, Roderick *Ghost Fields of Norfolk* (Larks Press) 2004

McLachlan, Ian & Zorn, Russell J. *Eighth Air Force Bomber Stories* (PSL 1991)

Smith David J. *Britain's Memorials & Mementoes* (PSL) 1992

Smith, Graham *Norfolk Airfields in the Second World War* (Countryside) 1994

South Norfolk Council *USAAF airfields in South Norfolk*

Stapfer, Hans-Heiri *Strangers In A Strange Land* (Squadron Signal) 1988

Walker, Peter M. *Norfolk Military Airfields* (Privately published) 1997